BYGONE BROMSGROVE

The pictures on the inside covers of this book are of Bromsgrove High Street in 1840. The characters depicted in the pictures are identified in Chapter Two.

TO

Jennie McGregor-Smith — without whose enterprise The Bromsgrove Society would not have been founded; without The Bromsgrove Society this book would not have been published.

ISBN 0 9509471 4 8

First published as a Special Limited Edition in 1981.

Reprinted 1982.

Second reprint 1985.

Third reprint and revised 1996

Since publication in 1981 some buildings identified by the names of the occupiers have changed hands; but it is hoped that the reader will still be able to work out their location.

Printed in England by Warwick Printing Co. Ltd., Warwick

BYGONE BROMSGROVE

An illustrated story of the town in days gone by

The Hop Pole Inn circa 1830 (Re-erected as Tudor House in New Road).

By Alan Richards with additional material by the Rev. W. Awdry, Jonathan Briggs, John Burman, Bill Kings, Robert Pancheri, John Weston and John Foster.

Edited by John Foster.

The Bromsgrove Society wishes to express its appreciation to all those who subscribed to the Special Limited Edition and so made publication possible.

It is especially grateful to those who have sponsored the book.

Personal Sponsors

Anonymous
Mr. and Mrs. Ian Arter
D. M. and C. Carrington
Tony M. Chance
Bernard K. Clements
J. S. Crawford
T. S. Frizzell
R. F. and L. M. Dent
N. J. Fisher
David Griffin
Miss M. D. and Messrs. L. H. and G. N. H. Hardy
Hilda M. Hewitt
Matthew Horton
Gordon F. and P. J. James
Roy and Ruth Lewthwaite
Mr. and Mrs. J. G. McGregor-Smith
The Misses J. E. and M. Messenger
Peter O'Connor
Michael Overton
Mr. and Mrs. Bernard Poultney
Peter Scott
J. S. Scott, T.D.
Ronald B. Searle
Gordon Selway
Councillor Mrs. Margaret Taylor
John Teece
D. A. and Ivy Tilt
Les Turner
J. C. Weston
Mr. and Mrs. R. B. Wharton
Dorinda Rae and Alfred A. Wood

Her Majesty the Queen has been pleased to accept copy number one of the Special Limited Edition of Bygone Bromsgrove.

Corporate Sponsors

Ansells Brewery, Birmingham
Badham & Grizzell (Butchers), 38, Worcester Road, Bromsgrove
Banks & Silvers, Tudor House, New Road, Bromsgrove
Bromsgrove Concrete Products Ltd., 231, Worcester Road, Bromsgrove
Bryant Properties Ltd., Solihull, West Midlands
Roger P. Dudley & Associates, The Coach House, Birmingham Road, Bromsgrove
L. G. Harris & Co. Ltd., The Brush Works, Stoke Prior, Bromsgrove
Lloyds Bank Ltd., Bromsgrove
Ottilie Hild School, College Road, Bromsgrove
Premier Glass Co. Ltd., Cox's Lane, Cradley Heath, Warley, West Midlands
Rainscourt Ltd., 110, High Street, Bromsgrove
Slater Yendall Ltd., Manufacturing Engineers, Park Farm Industrial Estate, Redditch
Norman Vine Ltd., Worcester Road, Bromsgrove
John B. Wilson & Sons Ltd., 133, High Street and Market Street, Bromsgrove

The following have helped the Society by purchasing books in quantity.

Birmingham Public Library
Bromsgrove Books, Worcester Road, Bromsgrove
Hereford and Worcester County Library
Hereford and Worcester County Schools in the Bromsgrove Area
J. C. Weston

CONTENTS

			Page
Foreword			7
Chapter 1.	On the Trail of Bromsgrove's Past	Alan Richards	10
Chapter 2.	Mid-nineteenth Century Bromsgrove	Alan Richards	42
Chapter 3.	Grafton Manor	John Weston	64
Chapter 4.	St. John's Church	Robert Pancheri	70
Chapter 5.	The Watermills of Bromsgrove	Jonathan Briggs	76
Chapter 6.	Nailmaking	Bill Kings	84
Chapter 7.	Canal Mania	John Burman	94
Chapter 8.	The Railway Revolution	Rev. W. Awdry	102
Chapter 9.	The Rise and Demise of Bromsgrove Guild	Robert Pancheri	118
Chapter 10.	The Court Leet and Court Baron of the Manor of Bromsgrove	John Foster	128
Bibliography			139
Index			140

Acknowledgements

A number of the illustrations are acknowledged in the text or below the pictures. We are most grateful for permission to reproduce them and also to the Birmingham Reference Library for facilities to reproduce many pictures from the Cotton Collection; also to Mr. Richard Harris who loaned us his print of the Hop Pole for the frontispiece. The goodwill of all these, and the many other unnamed people, who have been eager to help with this project is gratefully acknowledged.

Foreword

This book is not, nor is it intended to be, a comprehensive academic history of Bromsgrove. It is an entertainment based securely on historical fact, laced with a little local legend, enlivened with innumerable anecdotes and decorated with some of the best of the huge variety of pictures which can be found by those who search diligently. There are several important aspects of Bromsgrove which are only briefly mentioned in this book. That is because they are already adequately covered in other publications.

The exact date when Bromsgrove School was founded is not known. But 'Bromsgrove School through Four Centuries' by Icely, with 'Bromsgrove in Exile' by David Walters, give a comprehensive and very readable history of it. Walters' story of how the school was saved from wartime extinction – but only just—should be read by all who were educated there. The Housman family are probably the best known of Bromsgrove's citizens and there are many books of biography about them. Of special interest to local people is John Pugh's 'Bromsgrove and the Housmans'.

St. John's Church is Bromsgrove's oldest building and readers may be referred to W. A. Cotton's history of it written in 1881 or to the present Church Guide. Robert Pancheri's chapter about it has been written in the mood of the rest of this book and should interest those who do not wish to digest a wealth of architectural detail. This too is the tone of his chapter on Bromsgrove Guild. For a book which has more illustrations the reader should study 'The Guild of Decorative Arts' by Barbara June Morrison, the daughter of Archibald Davies who worked with him at the Guild. The chapter about the Railway by the Rev. W. Awdry was offered by him because he wanted to put the record straight on several matters which have been the subject of ill-informed reporting. The Society has been fortunate to attract a contribution from a man of such stature both in the field of literature and amongst steam train enthusiasts.

Bill Kings is the acknowledged expert on the nail industry which dominated the town for so long and it is important to have set down the tale he tells so engagingly to local organisations. Enthusiasts too tell of our watermills and of our canal. Had the importance of our mills to Bromsgrove been better appreciated stronger efforts might have been made to preserve Townsend Mill which at the date of writing is quite derelict. Amongst canal lovers Tardebigge's locks are nationally famous.

Bromsgrove in recent times has not had an aristocratic leader for its community. Hewell Grange which was occupied by the Lord of the Manor is now a Borstal; but it was always more readily identified with Redditch as was Hagley Hall with Stourbridge. A house which for many centuries must have been considered the home of the local squire is Grafton Manor. Unseen, tucked away down a long private road, it will be familiar only to those who patronise it in its present guise as a high class restaurant. A chapter about it fills an obvious need. Bromsgrove, with a few other places, has retained the tradition of a Court Leet. It provides a link between much of the rest of the history recorded in this book. It reminds us that history is colourful and enjoyable. When on Fair Day, children see the procession and the ritual ale-tasting and bread-weighing and they ask 'What is it all about?' they may be answered by the final chapter in this book.

Alan Richards started this whole venture off by sending to me a copy of a 'Town Trail' he had prepared for his students. It contained so much good material so well presented that it clearly deserved a wider audience. He has now added to that a lively picture of life in the town in Great Grandma's day — or if you are on the young side a bit before that!

Many people, too numerous to mention, have helped with this project; but it would be churlish not to acknowledge the substantial support I have had from an 'Editorial Board' of Miss Barley, our librarian, Tim Brotherton and John Weston together with Alan Richards, who, besides his major contribution, has helped me greatly with expert advice. Sheila Richards, Alan's wife, undertook that time consuming task – the preparation of the index.

The publication would not have been possible without the goodwill of the sponsors listed. And indeed of all those who subscribed in advance to the Limited Edition which has been the financial basis for what would otherwise have been a very speculative enterprise. I trust the faith of all these people will be rewarded by a product which they find satisfying and enjoyable.

John Foster
Editor – September 1981

Chapter One

On the Trail of Bromsgrove's Past

by Alan Richards

Sergeant Wright, Bromsgrove's rent collector in about 1830.
He lived at the corner of Hanover Street and St. John's Street.
From a water colour in the Cotton Collection by J. H. Scroxton.

1

This chapter is designed as a trail into Bromsgrove's past, following visual clues which can be found by walking around this old market town. In giving some accounts of the people and events associated with its oldest buildings it is hoped that a picture of Old Bromsgrove will emerge as clear as this description of the town in 1851 in a poem by J. H. Scroxton:–

> We have makers of buttons and makers of nails;
> Builders of coaches for roads and for rails;
> Artists in leather, in mortar, in wood;
> Artists in paint – both indifferent and good;
> Makers of candles, soap, soda, and salt;
> Concocters of drinks, both from crabs and from malt;
> Constructors and menders of watches and clocks;
> Repairers and vendors, and pickers of locks;
> We have sowers and reapers and grinders of grain;
> And dispensers of food both for stomach and brain;
> Manufact'rers of bread, pastry, butter and cheese;
> And makers of verses far better than these;
> We have some who teach music, and some who can draw,
> Expounders of gospel, exponents of law;
> We have men who write sermons, and men who write books;
> For ailing, we've doctors, for healthy we've cooks;
> We have some who can lecture, and some who can speak;
> And some who can gabble both Hebrew and Greek;
> We have schools for the lofty, and schools for the low;
> Both nurs'ries of virtue and nurs'ries of woe;
> We have drunkards and sober, both good men and bad;
> Some wise, and some foolish, some sane and some mad;
> We have dealers in gossip, detraction and lies,
> Who feast upon carrion, like maggots and flies;
> We have men who are honest and upright and true,
> And those who in gaol long penance should do.

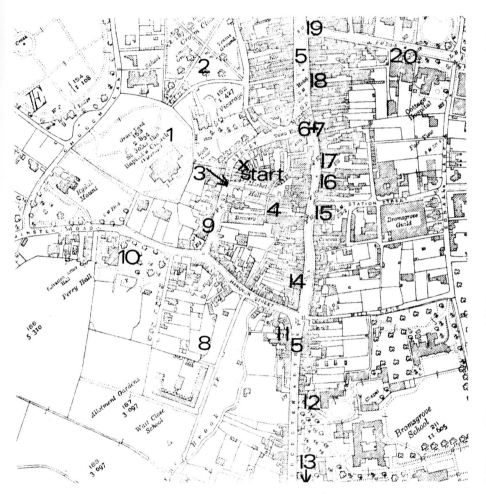

The numbers on this plan of Bromsgrove refer to the section headings in the text of the "Town Trail".

The section numbers which follow refer to the numbers on the plan of Bromsgrove facing page 10.

1. The hill with St. John's Church

The church is the oldest building in Bromsgrove built in local sandstone mainly in the thirteenth century, and its fourteenth century spire dominates the area, especially when approaching from the Lickey Hills. The oldest manor court records were kept in the spire until about 1728. The hill was probably the site of the earliest fortified settlement in Bromsgrove with a good water supply from the Spadesbourne which may have fed a moat round the hill. It also dominated the saltway from Droitwich northwards and the cattle droving road from Wales to the Midlands which came along the present Kidderminster Road.

The church is surrounded by a splendid belt of lime trees which were planted in 1792. There were originally 62 trees planted, the same number as the number of the church steps; but both have since been reduced. In the war against the Danes in Mercia in the early tenth century, King Alfred's daughter Ethelflaeda built a burh at Bromsgrove, one of a chain of hills fortified against the Danes. A burh was a pallisaded rampart of earthworks and was probably the hill on which the church stands. The poet Facer described the view of St. John's well:–

> Within the county's large extensive bound
> There's not a churchyard known or can be found
> With such a pathway so completely found;
> Full sixty trees whose branches far extend,
> O'erspread the way, from summer's heat defend;
> Prevent the rain, draw forth the breeze,
> With zephyrs passing through those spreading trees,
> Whose grove-like aspect to the distant eye,
> And in the midst a spire ascending high,
> The traveller admires when passing by;
> A view like this, perhaps he had not seen,
> Where'er his travels formerly had been.

The lychgate at the top of the steps was built during Cromwell's rule and the date, 1656, can be seen on the roof beam.

Inside on one of the oldest tombs is an important clue about the nature of life in early Bromsgrove. It is a carved boar's head, on which Sir Humphrey Stafford's head rests on his monument. According to one local legend about a jovial hunter, Sir Humphrey of Grafton Manor killed a wild

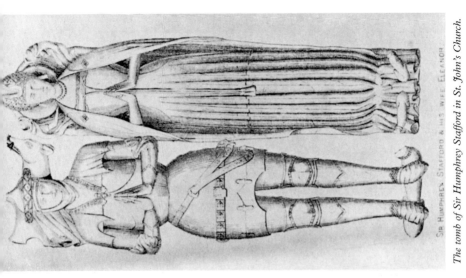

The tomb of Sir Humphrey Stafford in St. John's Church.

This is the old merchant's house which was demolished and moved to Avoncroft Museum of Buildings. (see page 26).

boar in order to free the Lady Alianora, who became his wife, from an enchantment. The carving of the boar in the church and the legend suggest that in the Middle Ages Bromsgrove was still part of a densely wooded area with few inhabitants except wild game. It was in fact part of the Royal Forest of Feckenham and subject to the harsh forest laws of the Middle Ages. In 1086 it is recorded in the Domesday Book that the manor of Bromsgrove contained a wood 7 miles long and 4 miles wide in which 4 nests of hawks were kept for breeding and training. It also contained 20 villeins, a reeve, a beadle, a priest, 92 cottagers, 9 serfs, one bondwoman and three watermills. Even with their families the population would only amount to a few hundred.

The last verse of one local ballad runs:

> In Bromsgrove Church the old lady lies,
> Well wind thy horn good hunter.
> There the wild boar's head is pictured by
> Sir Rylas the jovial hunter.

St. John's Church also contains other fine tombs of leading families in Bromsgrove, the Talbots and the Lyttletons.

Bromsgrove was surrounded by wild moorland still recalled in the place names Sidemoor, Wildmoor and Bournheath. The wild boar has been taken as the badge of Bromsgrove and used on seals.

It has been suggested that Bromsgrove's name was once Boarsgrove, but the town was called Bremesgrafa in Anglo-Saxon charters and Bremesgrave in the Domesday Book. Probably it owes its name to a great Saxon chieftain called Brem or Brom and Bremesgrave meant the grave or grove of Brem. Brem meant famous and renowned in Saxon times and the place may have been celebrated on account of the deeds of a great Saxon leader. He probably also gave his name to Birmingham, spelt Bromicham and Bremingham in the past and still locally called 'Brummagem'. There may be the same explanation for the names West Bromwich and Castle Bromwich.

2. Crown Close, the old Glebe Fields

Crown Close, the relatively open space between the church and Market Street, can be seen in the picture facing this page as it was in 1853. On the left of the church is the old vicarage which was built in 1848 and which is now used as a nursing home. The vicarage once stood alone in the middle of glebe fields provided to maintain the parson. On the right can be seen the National School (now offices) which was built in 1833. It was here that

THE CENTENARY OF KING EDWARD VI GRAMMAR SCHOOL, BIRMINGHAM.— JUNE 8, 1852 AT THE OPENING OF CROWN CLOSE.

Crown Close.

most of Bromsgrove's children were educated in the nineteenth century. Notice particularly the position of the church clock in the picture and compare it with its position on the spire today. The year before the picture was drawn the steeple was struck by lightning during a service causing the congregation, including many Sunday School children, to flee in panic through Crown Close. As a result a lightning conductor was attached to the steeple in 1853. Crown Close remained a fairly quiet backwater of Bromsgrove until the Western relief road was constructed in 1977.

Crown Close once contained a large fish pond called the George Pool or the Tinpool, and bowling green and gardens which belonged to the Crown Inn in the early nineteenth century. The Crown was probably the most important coaching inn in the town. Most of the 30 coaches which passed daily through Bromsgrove stopped there and the horses of the coaches between Birmingham and Worcester were changed at the Crown. The internationally renowned botanist, Benjamin Maund F.L.S., established his botanic garden in Crown Close and most of the illustrations for his much sought after books were painted by his sister and daughters in a house in Church Street. There is a memorial tablet to Maund in St. John's Church. There is a tradition that the Crown was once a religious house. Some evidence to support this was found when part of the inn was taken down in the nineteenth century and timbers were found carved in the ecclesiastical style. Other clues are that Church Street was once called Holy Lane and another lane leading into Crown Close was called Nun's Lane.

The churchyard which adjoins Crown Close contains many fine sandstone gravestones. The most visited are the two erected to the railwaymen. The story of their death is told in chapter 8.

3. Some of the oldest footpaths radiate from St. John's Church

One of the oldest footpaths leads from St. John's steps through Little Lane and up what is now Station Hill towards Finstall. Another across Crown Close and through Clegg's (formerly Dipple's) Entry crosses the High Street into the passage by Baylis's Shop. This was still being used as a public footpath into Ednall Lane in the nineteenth century. St. John's has been compared to the hub of a wheel with the radiating paths as spokes and the road running round it as the rim.

4. The Spadesbourne Brook and the Bromsgrove Flood

A bridge now carries St. John's Street traffic over the brook. Until 1829 there was no bridge and people had to use stepping stones set in the bed of the stream. The Spadesbourne, sometimes called the 'Town Brook', rises in the Lickey Hills. A plaque marks the level of the Bromsgrove Flood of 1792. It is set in a wall by the bridge in St. John's Street. Nash in his History of Worcestershire gives the following account of this flood:- 'On Friday, the 13th of March, 1792, there happened the most sudden and violent inundation ever known. In the afternoon of the same day, between the hours of three and four o'clock during a storm accompanied with loud and repeated claps of thunder, and the most vivid flashes of lightning, a water spout fell upon that part of the Lickey which is nearest to Bromsgrove. The day was sultry, the wind north-west; the quantity and violence of the water were so great that it swept all before it, hedges, gates, barns and houses. It carried a wagon heavily laden with skins and a large piece of timber down the street. The flood was so sudden that the inhabitants had no time to secure anything; the water was five feet deep in the street and covered the counters of the shops; many horses, cows and pigs were drowned; many of the stables were six or seven feet deep in water, and some children were lost. The spout burst about a mile and a half from Bromsgrove, near which place and at the upper part of the Lickey, there was only very moderate rain.'

Crane, the self-styled 'Bird of Bromsgrove' in the early nineteenth century describes the flood vividly in the following poem:

> The thievish stream, quite unawares
> Broke in, and stood to no repairs;
> Seven feet in depth came foaming down
> In open day, to take the town;
> Bore things away with swift dispatch,
> With everyone 'twas watch and snatch,
> Bawling and screaming out, stop, stop
> My timber! catch my pail and mop;
> My table with the tea things on,
> My heart is broke, my china's gone!
> My pigs, my malt will all be spoiled,
> Shut my malt-house! oh, save my child!
> To see the vessels setting sail,
> Loaded with spirits, wines and ale,
> Even mighty men were turning pale;
> In every vein their blood ran chill
> And women's tongues for once stood still.

The brook has dominated much of the life of Bromsgrove in the past, providing water for power for its mills, water for washing and until the late 1800s it acted as the town's open sewer.

5. The High Street

King John granted a market to Bromsgrove to be held everyTuesday. He also granted two fairs to be held on 24th June and 1st October (see section 8). During the two fairs and every market day, all the houses in High Street had the right to put up a stall in front of it 'extending to the channel'. House owners who erected these stalls paid the bailiff the 'pitching penny' as it was called 'they keeping the pitching in repair'. Pens were also attached to rings in the walls of the houses and were hired for the day. Most houses had high iron railings to protect them from cattle.

It is interesting to compare High Street today with the pictures inside the covers of this book. Chapter 2 does this in some detail but it will be noted that the Golden Cross is still a landmark though it has been rebuilt. An important change is the absence of New Road from the picture as it was not made until 1865.

In 1540 Leland described Bromsgrove as 'one very long strete, standynge on a playne ground. There is once a week a metely market. The town standeth somewhat by clothing. The harte of the town is metely well paved.' Dugdale in his book 'New British Traveller' described Bromsgrove in the year 1819 as 'a large and dirty place, full of shops and manufactories of needles, nails, sheeting and other coarse linen. In the principal street there are some good houses, while many of the more ancient buildings are wood, strangely decorated with black stripes and other unusual ornaments.' One of these buildings can be seen at the junction of High Street and St. John's Street. The timbers and its patterns were completely plastered over in the nineteenth century and were uncovered in 1910 when the shop was occupied by Mr Appleby, an ironmonger. The picture facing this page was drawn by Mr Wallace-Hadrill, a master at Bromsgrove School, and is reproduced by kind permission of his son. The left hand side of the building has been replaced by a modern one but it is of interest that in 1980 it was occupied by a solicitor, Mr. Holyoake, and one of his ancestors, John Holyoake Junior, was a solicitor in St. John's Street in 1840.

6. The Old Salt Track, Roman Road and Coaching Road

A clue to the age of the road through Bromsgrove from south to north is given in the print inside the front cover. The Lickey Monument can be seen with the High Street running straight towards it. By standing on the junction of St. John's Street with Worcester Road it is possible to see the Lickey Hills on the horizon, though the Monument is obscured by trees now. From the Birmingham Road, however, from Davenal House to All Saints Church, the

A pen and ink drawing of St. John's Street in the 1940s. By F. Wallace-Hadrill.

line of the road runs as straight as an arrow to the Lickey Monument, only bending to the west at All Saints. Archaeologists have traced the line of the Roman road from that point along the Spadesbourne Brook through Crows Mill, Lickey End and Long Eye and Linehouse Farm to the Lickey.

The Romans were probably not the first to build a straight road through Bromsgrove for they often followed the lines of ancient tracks. This one may be part of one of Britain's ancient leys (or tracks) which were marked by mounds, hills and stones as sighting points. The hill on which St. John's stands may have been one of these sighting points along a route which ran in a line from Birmingham over Selly Oak Hill, Rainbow Hill in Worcester, crossing the Severn at the Cathedral Ferry and then straight on again to the Malvern Herefordshire Beacon. This line can be easily traced using the Ordnance Survey 1/50,000 scale map (or the 'one inch'). The existence of the old Upper Saltway leading from Droitwich through Bromsgrove has long been recognised, and Watkins has traced the straight salt track from Droitwich southwards to Herefordshire Beacon via the long stretch of Rainbow Hill, crossing the Cathedral Ferry, through Lower Wick, crossing old Powick Bridge and through Burston Cross.

Two large boulders in the High Street may be ancient marking stones on the track as similar ones have been found on other suspected 'ley lines'. These boulders, each several tons in weight, stood in front of the Town Hall in the High Street until 1806 when new pavements were made. It seemed impossible to move them so large holes were dug beneath them into which they fell. Two more such boulders stood at the junction of Birmingham and Stourbridge Roads and these were removed to the main entrance to the Cemetery. It is of interest that no other beds of stone similar to these exist in the Midlands and according to geologists they come from Snowdonia. Whilst the origin of the straight track through Bromsgrove may be conjectural, it is probable that salt was being carried through the town from Droitwich before Roman times. By Edward I's time in the thirteenth century Bromsgrove Manor was sending 300 cartloads of wood annually to the Droitwich salt furnaces and receiving 3,000 bushels of salt in exchange

.

7. The Market Place and site of the old Town Hall

Bromsgrove's Town Hall stood at the junction of St. John's Street and Worcester Road in the middle of the old Market Place. The stalls of the open market were in front of the Town Hall and at its rear on market days. The old Town Hall was timber framed and looked very much like the town hall at Ledbury which has been preserved. It stood on oak pillars, the

John Cotton's sketches of old Bromsgrove. That of the old Town Hall which was pulled down in 1832 was drawn from the memories of others.

staircase being exposed to view; it is sketched in the picture facing page 20. It was demolished in 1832 and replaced by the town hall building which can be seen in the print inside the back cover; that was demolished in 1930.

The wool for Bromsgrove's important clothing industry was stored in the town hall, and when this was full in barns and stables nearby. The following handbill shows that wool could only be weighed on the scales provided by the bailiff at the town hall:

"June 24th, 1777 – Bromsgrove Fair.

The sellers and dealers in wool are desired to observe that the Town Hall is reserved for their use during the time of the fair, Scales and weights are likewise provided by the order of the bailiff of the said town. Therefore all persons are hereby required to weigh wool according to ancient custom at such scales only as appointed by his discretion."

The earliest stocks in the town of which anything is known were situated underneath the Town Hall on the right hand side of the entrance to the Market Place until 1832. The stocks were made of oak and a whipping post was attached to them. There were also stocks at the top end of the town where Birmingham Road starts. Drunkards were punished by being sentenced to six hours in the stocks in the seventeenth century and beggars were flogged at the whipping post. On 6th February 1824 James Jones and John Brown were publicly whipped for stealing a kettle. A pillory also stood in front of the Town Hall and the last person to be put in it was Michael Crockett for fraud in 1806. The nearest gibbet for hanging criminals seems to have been on the Lickey Hills between the church and the vicarage on the old coaching road. Highwaymen and robbers infested the wooded area of the Lickeys and often held up coaches there. One of the upright posts of this gibbet was still standing until about 1830 when it was used in a cottage fireplace on the Lickey to carry the chimney.

The Town Hall was the scene for the hiring fair which was held on 23rd September each year. Labourers and servants assembled in front of the George Inn next to the Town Hall to obtain jobs for the following year. Their occupation was indicated by the wearing of tokens. For example a carter wore a piece of whip cord in his hat and a cowman a lock of cow hair. Next the Town Hall was Roundabout Mill which was probably one of the three mills recorded in the Domesday Book.

8. Watt Close, the site of Bromsgrove's fairs and Cotton Mill

Watt Close, or Water Close, was the site of Bromsgrove's annual fairs on 24th June and 1st October. Horses for sale were trotted up and down the High Street on Fair Days. The October Fair was discontinued after the cattle market opened in 1853 on the site now occupied by a store next to the Recreation Road/Market Street car park.

The custom of 'crying the fair' was carried out until 1853 and the following proclamation was read out at the Town Hall and at the Fair:

"Oh yes! Oh yes! Oh yes! The High Bailiff of Bromsgrove to the Lord of the Manor of Bromsgrove, doth charge and command all persons that are here this day, that they do not bear, or wear any unlawful weapon, or make any assault, or riot or route, in disturbance of the presence of God and our Sovereign Lord the King, but as far as in them lies preserve the same, and that all sellers of cattle, sheep, pigs and horses, do pay to the toll gatherers the accustomed tolls, and that all sellers of wool do place the same in the place appointed for that purpose and that they do pay to the toll gatherers the accustomed tolls, immemorably collected, or they will answer to their peril.

God Save the King,
The Lord and Lady of the Manor,
The Bailiff of Bromsgrove,
And all loyal subjects."

A cotton mill, formerly known as 'the Buck House', used to stand at the lower end of Watt Close and was used as a cholera hospital during the 1832 epidemic. At the beginning of the nineteenth century it employed 200 to 300 people in the manufacture of linen cloth. The neighbouring fields used to be covered with the cloth while it was being bleached. Several of the houses in Hanover Street were used as weaving shops. This is a reminder that Bromsgrove made some of the best linen in Britain and as early as Henry VIII's time in the sixteenth century, clothing manufacture was Bromsgrove's chief industry. By that time many Bromsgrovians were employed in spinning, carding and sorting all kinds of wool, while others were weavers, fullers, shearmen and dryers. Let John Crane sum up the importance of the industry:

"Cloth spread upon the bleaching ground,
Flax growing all the country round,
Some spun by steam and some by hand,
No better yarn in all England,
Before all others sure to sell,
The Bromsgrove flaxen wears so well."

9. The buildings in St. John's Street

The row of buildings from St. John's steps to Kidderminster Road deserves a closer look. One of the finest eighteenth century houses adjoining the steps is now offices. It was once owned by Bromsgrove School and used to house the bachelor masters. Between this and the Shoulder of Mutton is one of the few remaining houses built mainly of local sandstone. Its gable is of square timber framing with brick infill and the beam is inscribed with the date 1674. The Shoulder of Mutton is one of Bromsgrove's oldest public houses though it was largely rebuilt in the late 1800s. Many of the meetings of the parish authorities were adjourned to the Shoulder of Mutton and so many parish matters were settled there. Opposite it used to be another inn, the Leg of Mutton. The 'Shoulder' was recorded as early as 1610 as a coaching inn and John Pugh says, in his book 'Bromsgrove and the Housmans', that he has been told that the caves in which the monks were reputed to have done their penance still existed behind the inn. There is a legend of a tunnel from Grafton Manor to the inn but there is no evidence which supports it. There is another that the inn is haunted by a ghost wearing a cloak. The father of the poet A. E. Housman used this pub frequently and would throw a stone on to the tin roof of an outbuilding at Perry Hall as a signal for the landlord to bring him a jug of ale.

10. Perry Hall – Home of the Housmans

Perry Hall, once the home of A. E. Housman, the poet, between 1859 and 1872, is just round the corner in Kidderminster Road. Although it has been extended to form the present hotel, the main building in which the Housman family lived is still intact and a good example of early nineteenth century architecture with its fine Gothic windows. It was rebuilt in 1824 by John Adams, a relative of the Housmans, owner of the Indigo Factory near Watt Close and the official Distributor of Stamps for North Worcestershire, equivalent today to a Customs and Excise Officer.

The ruins of an earlier seventeenth century Perry Hall built in sandstone with mullioned windows can be seen in the grounds. Laurence Housman in his autobiography describes Perry Hall in John Adams day as a house 'containing many thousands of pounds worth of government property that it might well have attracted thieves. For which reasons ponderous fittings had been provided in all directions against burglary; office windows heavily barred, a back door three inches thick, studded with nails, and with a huge lock that turned twice, shutters in the living rooms that rose up from the bowels of the earth and were locked in place by an elaborate combination of cross-bars and screws, swing bells on passage doors, and up on the roof an alarm bell waiting to be rung. And though in our day the place no longer contained property of much value, the ritual of shutter-closing still went on, and a hefty job it was for the maids, filling the house each evening with rumblings'. The original front door remains as witness to these precautions against burglars, nailstudded and with a great lock; there is a square peephole cut in the upper part of it.

John Adams owned the land opposite right up to the church wall and for this reason the hill became known as Adams Hill.

11. The Black Cross

Amongst many public houses in Bromsgrove the Black Cross has the oldest building. It has been standing at the four cross roads of Worcester Road, Hanover Street and Hill Lane since the early seventeenth century. It is a timber framed building in its upper storey whilst its ground floor has been rebuilt in brick on the sandstone foundations. It has a good diamond pattern in the timber frames of its left hand gable. The inn sign with its black cross is not a common one and W. A. Cotton in his booklet 'The Old Houses of Bromsgrove' suggests the origin of the name may lie in the old custom of burying the bodies of those whose deeds were black at the cross roads. The black cross with golden edges is also the sign of the Teutonic Knights. There is a tradition that King Charles, after his defeat at the Battle of Worcester in 1651, hid himself behind a large open chimney in the kitchen of the inn. It was a coaching inn and a wooden door set at coach roof height in the side of the inn was probably used for loading coaches.

Battlefield Brook joins the Spadesbourne just below the Black Cross. This and Battlefields Farm on the Kidderminster Road get their name because of a skirmish there by patrols during the Battle of Worcester. There is a story that a prisoner was put into a niche in the sandstone wall on the roadside near Park Gate and shot at with a cannon, which missed him but left a hole which can still be seen.

12. Bromsgrove School, formerly called the King Edward VI Grammar School

Nearly opposite the Black Cross is Bromsgrove's oldest school. Its oldest building can be seen through the entrance gates. It was built in 1695 by Sir Thomas Cookes when he refounded the school. It was about this time that it moved to its present site. Before that the Town Hall had served as a schoolroom. To the left of the entrance gates is an eighteenth century building which was restored in 1979. By looking carefully at the drawing facing page 31 which shows the end of this building, the exact position of the timber framed houses shown in the picture can be identified. They were demolished after the Second World War.

13. Early Victorian cottages in the Worcester Road
Just below the school on the same side of the road is the best row of terraced early nineteenth century cottages still standing in Bromsgrove with steps leading down the bank on which they were built. Then this area was a rough neighbourhood with nailers living on both sides of the road. Their huge consumption of beer was well catered for by a number of public houses, of which the Turks Head and the Britannia remain.

14. Worcester Road
Walking back from Hanover Street along the Worcester Road towards the High Street is Bromsgrove's most intact row of Victorian shops, the buildings of which, apart from the shop fronts, have changed little in the last 100 years. The Dog and Pheasant is one of the oldest public houses but it was rebuilt at the end of the nineteenth century, and suffered more renovation later. Next to it, nearer the High Street, is a much altered building of the eighteenth century which is full of character.

15. Bromsgrove House
Opposite, on the corner of Station Street adjoining Neale's garage, is the site of the oldest timber framed building in Bromsgrove, a merchant's house, which was removed to Avoncroft Museum of Buildings. The house occupied a good position in medieval Bromsgrove looking across the village green towards the church. Facing page 12 there is a photograph of it when it was still standing there taken in about 1914. The drawing by John Cotton on page 21 shows the rear and side view from Station Street. The Sampson Inn then stood opposite on the corner of Little Lane and on the other corner of Station Street was the Wheatsheaf. It is of interest that the site now occupied by Neale's garage was at one time a wheelwright's.

16. Sandstone Building
Just above Station Street is one of the most interesting old buildings when viewed from the side and rear. It is another of the few houses left built in sandstone with some brick additions. It was much altered in the nineteenth century when its front was completely rebuilt with the facade higher than the

original roofline. Part of the building was probably built in the sixteenth century. It has a timber framed passage running through it. It is not easy to get a view of this building from the back; but it is well worth the effort.

17. The Golden Lion

Above the sandstone building was a charming old coaching inn, the Golden Lion, which has now been converted to offices. It is eighteenth century with distinctive Venetian type windows, with Gothic central lights with ogee heads. It has a classical doorway with pillars and a pediment. There was a dovecote at the rear on the gable end.

Feargus O'Connor, the Chartist leader, signed the land deal in this inn which led to the Chartist Settlement at Dodford. Several of the Chartist bungalows are still standing there.

The Golden Lion stood on the site of a manor house, The Manor of Diocese or Dyers. This was pulled down in 1777 when Thomas Andrews built the inn.

18. The Golden Cross

The 'Cross' was rebuilt in 1932 but is on the site of one of the town's oldest coaching inns. When the railway was opened in 1840 a horse bus carried passengers from the Golden Cross to the station and a bell was pulled to tell the passengers that the bus was departing. Both bus and bell can be seen in the print inside the front cover. This hotel was the headquarters of the Conservatives during the Parliamentary elections of the nineteenth century, which were often more riotous and violent than they are today. The bye-election of 1859 was particularly exciting in Bromsgrove when a mob attacked the 'Cross' and the cavalry had to be called out. By midday of polling day the tradesmen had already put up their shutters because of the stone throwing which had broken many windows. At 3 p.m. the mob broke through the gates to the yard which was at the back of the inn, and where the Conservatives had their committee rooms. The twenty-four constables who had been stationed in the yard managed to close the gates again after a struggle. The Riot Act was then read out from the first floor of the Crown Hotel, but the rioting still continued.

Another pitched battle took place during the afternoon between the mob of several hundreds and fifty of the older boys from Bromsgrove School who had marched out of the school wearing the scarlet Conservative colours. The boys were forced back to the school and the stabling at the 'Cross' was used as an ambulance station to treat the injured. Birmingham was telegraphed for help and 120-150 cavalry. After the police had failed to quell the rioting, and one voting station had been forced to close down for an hour, the Dragoons withdrew their swords from their scabbards, charged at the mob and dispersed them.

The number who had the right to vote at that election was only just over 4,000 and they could be 'got at' in a number of ways. One Bromsgrove nailmaster brought ten voters in a waggon to the Golden Cross, close to the polling booth. They were supplied freely with drink, some of which was also drugged, to prevent them voting. Two were so over-drugged that a doctor had to be called to pump out their stomachs.

19. The Hop Pole Inn

Just off High Street, up New Road, is one of Bromsgrove's outstanding landmarks which has been used in a stylised form as the badge for the Bromsgrove Society. It is pictured in the frontispiece to this book as it was before it was demolished to make way for the construction of New Road in 1865. The upper part of the present building is a more faithful reconstruction of the old Elizabethan building than the ground floor whose windows and porch were designed by the Victorian architect in charge of the rebuilding. The original Elizabethan building was built by William Brooke and his initials can be seen still on the centre gable. It was in the possession of the Brooke family from 1572 to 1825 and was considered one of the finest examples of Elizabethan timber framed houses in the country. Our picture is from Habershon's book, published in 1836, The Ancient Half-Timbered Houses in Britain, in which he called it 'the most beautiful piece of street architecture in Bromsgrove, with rich carving on each of its gables and with the timber frames curiously decorated with scallops, flowers and leaves, and has good effect'.

The headquarters of Charles I's army were at Bromsgrove on 11th May 1645 during the civil war and many soldiers were probably quartered at the Hop Pole before proceeding to Hawkesley House. There is also the following description of the assembly of troops, led by Sir Gilbert Talbot, in front of the Hop Pole Inn, before they joined King Charles II's army at the battle of Worcester in 1651. 'The bells rang merrily in the fine old tower, from the battlements of which a banner, bearing the Red Cross of St. George, was floating in the summer breeze; in the open space in front of the Market Hall a mast was fixed in the ground, from which hung a large flag, bearing the Royal Arms; from various windows colours were suspended among which the proud banner of Sir Gilbert Talbot, bearing a huge golden lion and his ancestral motto "Fiat voluntas tua" were very prominent; at another window of the fine old timber house (the Hop Pole) hung the banner of Sir Thomas Lyttleton, of Frankley, at another the Banner of Sir Thomas Cookes, of Bentley; of several of the neighbouring gentry, among which were those of the Vernons, Bearcrofts, Noels, Fields, Grants, Sheldons, Fones and many others were visible. The good town presented, what with the sound of music, the flash of sunlight upon armour, the prancing of steeds, the constant bustle attendant upon such an assemblage, the confused sound of voices, and the various groups in which they were disposed, formed quite a holiday appearance, and seemed rather a gathering for merry-making, than an assemblage of men upon an errand of blood and death. The wine flowed freely, the roystering song was raised here and there, the gaiety of assured success sat upon all parties, and not a cloud seemed to dim the enjoyment of the house. There was a slight movement in front of the old house, and the leaders of the little party came forth, mounted their horses, and as the clock struck noon, Sir Gilbert Talbot, placing himself at their head, in a loud voice shouted: "Now gentlemen, for God and King Charles". The ranks were formed and away they started, many of them never to return again.'

20. The Devil of Bromsgrove

Walk up New Road and on the right hand side was a red terracotta figure of a horned Devil on the gable end of the Victorian School of Science and Art. It has not been possible to discover why it was put there, but it is known that there was quite an outcry in the town at the time about what was considered a most inappropriate piece of decoration for a seat of learning. An entertaininigly imaginative explanation for its presence was, according to a local sporting journalist, Loppylugs, given by Mr. Frank Holyoake who practised as a solicitor in Bromsgrove from 1878 to 1944. 'The Rousler', he explained, 'lived on the Lickey Hills and used to fly down to Bromsgrove to see his old friend the Bromsgrove Boar. One bitterly cold winter night, in thick fog, it lost its way and landed on the gable of the Institute. It became frozen and has stayed there ever since'. The figure can now be seen in Bromsgrove library.

Just above the Institute was the Cottage Hospital, a good example of a Victorian Building in the Tudor style designed by John Cotton and built in 1891. These buildings have now been replaced by flats. Some of the features of their facades have been retained in the new building.

Old houses near to Bromsgrove School which are now demolished.
Drawn by William A. Green.

The tithe barn, later used as a theatre. The site was subsequently used for a cinema and then a bingo hall.
From an engraving in the Cotton Collection.

The next set of section headings refer to the plan facing page 32.

21. Two Shops on the corner of New Road and High Street

The eighteenth century building, next to the Hop Pole in the print inside the front cover, is still standing. One has one of the oldest Edwardian shop fronts in the town, though quite different to the bay windows with small panes which it had in 1840 and which can be seen in the print.

22. The old Sow and Pigs

At the corner of High Street and Church Street, on a site now occupied by offices, once stood one of Bromsgrove's oldest taverns. It was called the Sow and Pigs in the nineteenth century but before that it was known as Dunklin's Mug House. Facing page 37 is a drawing of the yard to these premises made by John Cotton in 1882 shortly before the timber framed upper storey was demolished. It is a good example of the many half timbered houses which still remained in Bromsgrove then with its pump, its precarious chimney, its latticed windows, and with its first storey built in local sandstone. William Cotton bought the Sow and Pigs in 1874 and it has been an auctioneer's offices ever since. The building shown in the drawing is the back of No. 3 Church Street and it is still standing, though much altered and renovated.

23. The old Tithe Barn in Church Street

At the bottom of Church Street stood the old Tithe Barn which was used to store the crops paid in tithe to maintain the parish priest. It was also used as a parish hall and theatre until it was demolished in 1844. Mrs. Siddons is said to have played here as the young daughter of Roger Kemble whose company of actors staged plays in the barn in 1765.

24. Rainscourt's and Lloyds Bank

Further up the High Street is the largest and most complete timber framed building in the town which was built in the early sixteenth century. Its timbers are close-studded, a sign that it was a building of high social status, probably first owned by a wealthy cloth merchant. At one stage of its long life it was the Unicorn Inn and the horns can still be seen on its gable peaks. It is jettied, that is projecting over the street, at second floor level. In contrast with this medieval style, next door is Lloyds Bank in the Georgian style with a fine classical stone portico and Doric columns. The building on the other side of Rainscourt's was built earlier than the bank, in the late eighteenth century.

25. Chapel Street

Through the precinct to Lloyds Bank are two good examples of Victorian buildings in the classical style. One is the United Reformed Church built in 1833 with its Greek Doric porch and long arched windows. The other is the former school of the chapel which was built in 1852 in red brick with arched windows. Chapel Street with its sandstone walls and Victorian style cottages provides one of Bromsgrove's most attractive streetscapes.

26. Passage opposite Lloyds Bank

Opposite the bank is a late seventeenth century building with a plaque giving the date 1699, and next to it an eighteenth century building with dormer windows and moulded pediments. The passage between them leads to a fine view of old Bromsgrove. Down the passage is an early seventeenth century timber framed building. Look back through the passage to see the classical portico of Lloyds and the fine timber framed black and white of Rainscourt's.

The views of the backs of roof tops of the houses in High Street starting from Mill Lane to the end of Crown Close give a clear impression of old Bromsgrove with ancient shops built on the front of narrow burgage plots and often narrow houses built on behind them. Many of these can only be seen by peering over the tops of the walls in Market Street. The boundaries of the plots have remained the same since the Middle Ages.

27. The Town Mill – Mill Lane

The name Mill Lane provides the clue to one of Bromsgrove's most important buildings in days gone by. It was the Town Mill which was one of the three mills recorded in the Domesday Book. It stood where a supermarket now stands. The mill was also known as King's Mill because James I reserved this mill and its rental to himself when he granted the Bromsgrove Manor to the Howes family in 1612. There were two bridges, one over the flood gates of the mill pond and one over the stream from the pond to the wheel – the 'wayne bridge' from High Street down Mill Lane.

The Ecclesiastical Commissioners sold the Town Mill and its pool to the Local Board of Bromsgrove who dried up the pool and demolished the mill in 1883. The demolition was recorded by John Cotton and is pictured facing page 53

The Local Board also diverted the course of the brook in 1883 and made a new street, Market Street, through the land of the old Rectory Manor House.

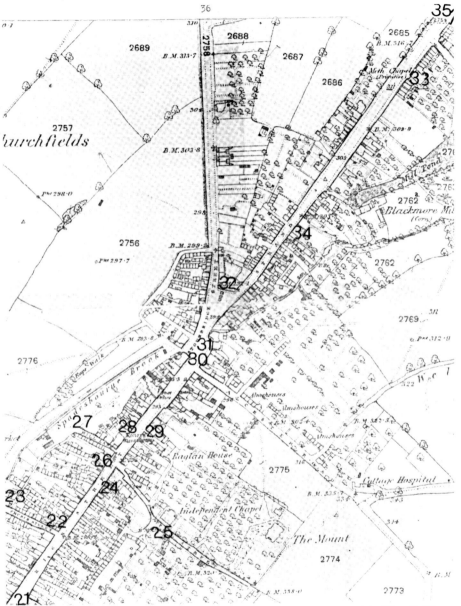

The numbers on this plan of Bromsgrove refer to the section headings in the text of the "Town Trail"

Sketch Elevation of the Old Manor House, High Street, Bromsgrove pulled down about the end of July or beginning of August 1921. The building was of stone, the gables plastered, the whole colored a buff tint, the lower part had been used as a shop and the bay windows were modern, also the sign. The door and frame were oak and old. The gables were timberframed and plastered over
(Rectory Manor)   John Cotton.

This was the old Manor House which was demolished to make way for Bryant's Garage, which in turn was demolished to make way for the Mill Lane Precinct.

28. The Rectory Manor House and the Racecourse

Just above Mill Lane in the High Street stood the Rectory Manor House, another very old sandstone house which was demolished in 1921 to make way for Bryants Garage. The Rectory Manor was originally part of Feckenham Forest, but long before the Reformation it was granted to St. Mary's Monastery Church at Worcester. A Court Baron was held there twice a year by the Prior of Worcester Convent. The tenant of the manor was bound to receive the Prior's cellarist and steward during this court at his own charges.

The land of Rectory Manor belonged to the Dean and Chapter of Worcester Cathedral in the nineteenth century who leased it to the Windsor family of Hewell Grange. Much of this land was used as a racecourse from 1840 to 1847. It extended from Church Street to what is now Parkside School playing fields. It was circular and almost a mile in length. Until 1792 horse racing also took part on land at Marlbrook still known as the Horse Course.

29. Peacocks stores – an elegant Georgian Building

Returning to the High Street and walking towards the Birmingham Road can be seen possibly the most elegant Georgian frontage in the town. Its roof has a low pitched pediment above a central window with a curved moulded head, and there are decorative pilasters at each side of the building.

30. The top end of High Street

Behind the very Victorian public house, the Queens Head, in the Crescent was the eighteenth century bell foundry of Richard Sanders and later of William Brooke. Sanders cast his first bell there in 1703 and about fifty of them are still in use in Worcestershire churches. One of his noted rings is in St. Helen's, Worcester, commemorating the Duke of Marlborough's victories. His trade mark was a plain cross and that of Brooke a bell.

Adjoining the Queens Head is a row of interesting buildings, which despite their Victorian appearance, could be much earlier timber framed buildings which were later enclosed in brick. One of these, the Mitre, was a centre for cider making in the nineteenth century. Now restored they are shops and offices with flats over.

121

about 1913 this property was sold by John Cotton to daughter B. Wilson. She moved the neighbours Mr H.J. Stone of the ward — his brother W.H. Wilson died and the property was sold by auction by Smith & Rimson when Mr A.E. Chappell bought it & the cottage adjoining in Church Street.

gable of Cattle Market Tavern

Dr Underhill owned these premises of times before Mr Wilson had them.

Back door of Mr J.C. Cotton's premises

E.B. Cotton bought this cottage but at his death it was bought by John B. Wilson from the Metropolitan Bank. Mr Wilson sold it by auction about 1913 when Mr A.E. Chappell auctioneer bought it.

6 March 26 1882

Sketch of the back of Premises No 3 Church St. Bromsgrove adjoining the Cattle Market Tavern. The lower story by pump belongs to me (J.C.) the upper part with the half timber work was pulled down and rebuilt soon after this sketch was made. The pump was removed and well filled up about the beginning of 1894.

John Cotton's sketch of a yard off Church Street.

31. The Crescent and the Strand

The eighteenth and early nineteenth century buildings in this part of the town give a strong impression of Bromsgrove as it was before all the rebuilding. Two shops (Nos. 146 and 148) are part of one eighteenth century house with five camber headed windows, stone quoins and a moulded stone cornice at the eaves. Just above here the Spadesbourne crosses the High Street underground. The old name, the Strand, which was the name of the lower part of Birmingham Road and which means the margin of land near a river, is a clue to the reason for the curve in the road at this point. It was probably dictated by the diagonal course of the brook across the street and the best place at which it could be forded.

32. The Old Workhouse and Tannery

At the junction of the Strand with Stourbridge Road (or Rotten Row as the lower part of Stourbridge Road used to be called) is an early eighteenth century building which dominates the top end of High Street. It was Bromsgrove's first workhouse until the new Union Workhouse was built in 1838. The front part of it was known as Cock Hall and was sold by John Southall to Bromsgrove Parish in 1723 when it was enlarged at the back and converted to the parish workhouse. Its first governor was Edward Long and in 1738 there were 35 inmates; in 1822 there were 45.

After the new Union Workhouse was built the old one became a tannery owned by a Mr. Tandy. The public weighing machine and keeper's house stood in front of it as is shown in the picture facing page 39. The weighing machine was placed there in 1796 and its first attendant received three shillings (15p) a week in wages. Out of the profits £20 a year was paid to the St. John's Sunday School and some of the profits were used to build an organ in St. John's and to pay an organist who replaced the string band which had provided music previously.

Tandy's Tannery is a reminder that tanning was an important industry in Bromsgrove and, because it caused bad smells, tanning could only be carried out at certain times. Queen Elizabeth I gave Bromsgrove a licence to carry on the trade between Michaelmas and Lady Day within 16 days and within 8 days at other times. Many curriers were prosecuted for leaving skins in the Spadesbourne and the old name of Rotten Row for the bottom of Stourbridge Road may derive from the stink of the tannery. Curriers and their knives for skinning animals were a common sight in Bromsgrove, and one of them was convicted of murdering a man with his knife under the Town Hall in 1819. The inscription on the late Tandy's house and Tannery.

Mrs Green's Nail warehouse.

W. Weaver builder

old weighing-machine office

gravestone of the murdered man, Thomas Manningly, in St. John's churchyard reads:

> Beneath this stone lies the remains,
> Who in Bromsgrove Street was slain,
> A currier with his knife did the deed
> And left me in the street to bleed.

At the back of Tandy's Tannery hides and leather were hung up. The building had unusual window shutters of sloping boards, which let in air and light but not rain. Mr. Tandy once put a barrel of beer outside his house and invited passers by to drink the health of his housekeeper who had just got married.

The building is now restored. This was done by Hortons, solicitors in the town for several generations.

33. The Birmingham Road – Stourbridge Road junction

Next to the tannery was the nailing warehouse of W. Green, probably Bromsgrove's most important nailmaster in the nineteenth century. It later belonged to another nailmaster, Eliza Tinsley. Many of the nailers lived in the Strand and Stourbridge Road as well as in Worcester Street. Nailers are recorded in the Bromsgrove Parish registers as early as 1672 and by a hundred years or so later nailmaking had replaced cloth weaving as the town's chief trade. Henry Ince was a nailer and a local Methodist Preacher. He came from Bournheath and exercised a strong moral leadership over the other nailers, leading them in eight strikes. He often preached at the Primitive Methodist chapel in Birmingham Road. It is still standing and was built in 1861. It now serves as H.Q. for the Royal British Legion locally. It was the nailers' chapel because eight of the original trustees were nailers. The nailers were so grateful to Henry Ince for his leadership during the 1869 strike they presented him with 'a frock coat, waistcoat and trousers, a silk hat, stockings, garters and a walking stick. After the presentation Mr. Ince retired and later appeared, attired from head to foot in his new suit. He met a most enthusiastic response' (From a report in the Bromsgrove Messenger).

34. The Birmingham Road to the Crabmill and Union Workhouse

The eighteenth century Davenal House (No. 28) was renovated by Dennis Norton and is now a doctors surgery. It has five bays and a classical doorway with Doric pilasters. The fine lead drainpipes and rainwater heads, each with an embossed boar's head, are the recent work of a local craftsman in lead, Mr. Hems. In 1850 it was owned by Mr. Thomas Day, who was clerk to the Board of Guardians responsible for running the Union Workhouse. The Workhouse was built in Georgian style in 1838 and after use as Health Service offices has been sold for commercial use.

All Saints Church was designed by John Cotton in the Gothic style and was erected in 1874. The old cattle pound at the corner of Burcot Lane was incorporated into the churchyard. The pound was used by the constable when he found stock grazing on roadside wastes, because the land was claimed by the Lord of the Manor.

Opposite is the Crabmill. This splendid eighteenth century inn has fine Venetian windows and a classical doorway. Its inn sign is one of the best in Bromsgrove. There was probably a cider mill attached to it powered by the nearby Spadesbourne.

According to local tradition, John Wesley, the founder of Methodism, stayed overnight at this inn on 11th September 1783 when he was 80 years of age. He recorded this visit to the Methodist Society of Bromsgrove in his journal and that he rode to the town in a chaise rather than on horseback, no doubt because of his advanced age. It is not known where the Methodists met before they built their first chapel in the Kidderminster Road in 1832, which was succeeded by their late Victorian church in New Road in 1883.

Author's Note to Chapters One and Two – The first two chapters of this book have been made possible by the work of some great Bromsgrovians. Many of the memories and scenes of Bygone Bromsgrove would not have survived without the careful recording of two Bromsgrove brothers, William A. Cotton and John Cotton, and their astonishing collection of material which is now preserved in the Birmingham Reference Library. Included in the Cotton Collection are the reminiscences of Dr. George Fletcher and G. Bradfield on which chapter two is largely based. These were published in the Bromsgrove Messenger between 28th December 1929 and 1st September 1930. Few local newspapers have printed so much local history as the 'Messenger'; and one editor, F. W. Harvey, was outstanding for his encouragement of writers of local history during his editorship between 1886 and 1940.

Despite the work of these Bromsgrovians of the past, this book would not have been published without the drive and enthusiasm of a living Bromsgrovian, John Foster. My final debt is to my wife who has shared in the research, and has done most of the typing, and to my daughter Elizabeth for typing.

Alan Richards,
BA.,Hons., London,
M.A.(Econ.Hist.) and M.A.(African Studies) Birmingham.

Chapter Two

Mid-Nineteenth Century Bromsgrove

by Alan Richards

Until the railways came Bromsgrove was a busy posting town for stage coaches.
From a water colour in the Cotton Collection by J. H. Scroxton.

2

Well peopled with inhabitants,
and plenty to supply their wants,
neat spirits, porter ales and wines,
over the doors in golden lines;
fowls, fishes, corn and famous meat,
our butcher's signs are good to eat.
A stream to wade through when it rain'd,
now neatly paved, and under-drained,
a coach in passing Bromsgrove streets
with accidents no longer meets,
no horses down upon their knees,
no broken bones, nor axle-trees;
the middle raised, the pathway good,
no reason now to fear a flood.
On foot a stranger now-a-days
looks upon it in amaze;
flagstones and pebbles, white and brown,
to walk on through this pretty town,
the length and breadth as I proceed,
of all the streets for you to read,
this would be troublesome indeed;
a spacious church and churchyard too,
an organ, just bespoke, quite new.

A thoroughfare, a place of trade,
the nails and needles that are made;
for lines and fish hooks, famous good,
this is the town and neighbourhood.
Crank-motions turn the money in,
our water goes to card and spin;
at combing wool is getting on,
will work the stocking frames anon.
Cloth spread upon the bleaching ground,
flax growing all the year around;
some spun by steam and some by hand,
no better yarn in all England.
What linen cloth comes up to ours?
Who else weaves landscapes, birds and flowers?
before all others sure to sell,
the Bromsgrove flaxen wears so well.
Machines are often made to wash,
Machinery begins to thrash;
will soon begin to plough and sow,
months after that will reap and mow,
do all the work in every trade
when folks by hand have nothing made.
Work cannot jade and teach us then.
No! we shall all be gentlemen.

(The Loyal, Ingenious and Flourishing Town of Bromsgrove by John Crane)

John Crane writing his poetry at the start of the nineteenth century described a town which was beginning to experience more rapid change than it had ever had in the past, with the introduction of better roads, canals and machines. These changes have been summed up as The Industrial Revolution, and by 1800 even a small market town like Bromsgrove was affected by it. Crane began with, perhaps, the most dramatic change in his day, the building of a better road through the town which had speeded up coach travel and the movement of goods. This was the turnpike road between Birmingham and Bristol with a toll house at the bottom of Rock Hill and another at Lickey End. Better roads like this had been made possible by the formation of the Turnpike Trusts in the eighteenth century. These bodies carried out road improvements and paid for them by building turnpike gates and tollhouses at which travellers had to pay tolls. There were tollhouses on other roads leading into Bromsgrove at Red Cross on the Kidderminster Road, at Lydiate Ash, at Hundred House on the Stourbridge Road, at Tutnall and at Stoke Heath. Crane described the raising of the level of High Street and the new flagstones so that it was no longer frequently flooded by the brook, horses no longer fell down holes and the axles of coaches were no longer broken. The repaving of High Street in 1806 no doubt inspired this poem. This main street had become so bad that the inhabitants of the town were threatened by an indictment on 26th May 1806. They raised £350 and the Turnpike Trust gave £150 to pay for the work.

Crane also listed the town's main industries and it is plain that the ancient cloth industry still flourished side by side with the nailing. The importance of the brook for power is also clear. More significantly for the future, Crane records that steam power was being used to spin flax, and that some local farmers were using threshing machines, which had been invented in the 1780s and which led to increased unemployment for farm workers. Was he the first to prophesy that machines would replace all manual labour and lead us into an age of leisure?

The two engravings which are at the beginning and end of this book have been dated by Dr. George Fletcher to 1840. They give a vivid glimpse into that early Victorian age. Some of Bromsgrove's leading citizens are depicted in the pictures and many of them have been identified by Dr. George Fletcher and his father. They present an elegant scene.

Looking at the picture of the High Street inside the back cover facing south towards the then new town hall (built in 1832) the old Crown Hotel stands out in the right foreground as the most important coaching inn, and an ostler is taking a horse into its yard. The name of this inn is still remembered in the name Crown Close. Almost opposite was the oldest coaching inn in Bromsgrove, the Hop Pole. The opening of the railway from Birmingham to Gloucester in 1840 had not yet destroyed the prosperity of Bromsgrove's coaching inns, but within a few years the Crown was forced to close and the Hop Pole was demolished in 1865 to make way for the new road to the station. It was rebuilt round the corner in New Road. Bentley's Directory of Worcestershire, published in 1840, saw what was to come. 'On the opening of the railway to Camp Hill which is expected very shortly, it is probable that most of the coaches between Worcester, Birmingham and Bromsgrove will be taken off the road. In January 1841, the Mails will be conveyed by the railway to the North and South.'

The shop next to the Crown belonged to the printers and booksellers, Maund and Palmer. Benjamin Maund was a clever scholar, who produced one of the most beautiful books on the flowers of Britain in the nineteenth century, and as a result became a Fellow of the Linnean Society. Alfred Palmer who started as an assistant to Maund soon became a partner. In 1860 Palmer began to publish the Bromsgrove Messenger from these premises, though only the front page was local and printed in Bromsgrove. There was also a well used subscription library in the front room of this shop. Benjamin Maund can be seen standing next to the first lamp post past his shop talking to a lady in a bonnet. Two masters from Bromsgrove School are standing outside Maund and Palmer's, wearing mortar boards and carrying canes. Next to Maund and Palmer the name Jefferies can be seen over the top of the shop. Mr. Jefferies, who was Chairman of the Town Council, had a large grocery shop with two frontages. Another grocer's was next door bearing the legend 'Griffin, tea dealer'. Mr. Griffin's son went to Miss Knight's school for small children with young George Fletcher. Next was Green's the chief shoemaker to Bromsgrove School. And then the Post Office with Mr. Johnson as Post Master. This must have been one of the smallest in the country. Situated adjoining Dipple's (now Clegg's) Entry it was only 9 feet wide and there was no access for the public from the street. Customers had to transact their business through a trap door about 18inches square. A draper, Mr. Cutler, who also did tailoring had another shop nearby.

In the foreground of the engraving a member of the gentry is driving northwards with his coachman and footman. On the left, standing outside his shop is Mr. Brown, a painter and plumber. He is wearing an overcoat and is talking to another tradesman wearing a top hat and apron. A huge roll of lead was always lying full length in the passage of Brown's. Next to the Hop Pole, on what is now the south corner of New Road and High Street was an auctioneer's business belonging to Mr. Steedman, then came Ward's, a baker. Mr. Amphlett, yet another grocer, a good man of business and very active, like his competitor Jefferies, in local affairs, was next door. A butcher's shop kept by Mr. Francis, who also farmed the Durrance at Upton Warren, was next and Partridge the butcher occupied this shop in the 1980s as his family had for very many years.

The very new gas lights are prominent in both engravings, and these were provided in the town by the Bromsgrove Gas and Light Company established only in 1836. By 1840 the lamplighter was a familiar figure in High Street, carrying a ladder which he had to climb to extinguish or light each lamp. They were lit for only seven months of the year and during the rest of the year people went about after dark at their own risk. Middle class people were having gaslight installed in their own homes by the 1840s. But Dr. George Fletcher said that his father refused to have gas in his house at the top of Church Street until 1858, and then only on the ground floor. Most people still lit their houses by candlelight.

In the picture of the High Street facing north, inside the front cover, and leading straight to the newly erected Lickey Monument (1834), the first shop in the foreground on the left is that of T. D. Thomas, the draper and undertaker. His shop was called Manchester House, no doubt because of the Manchester made cotton goods which he sold. When his shop was demolished in 1897, the new building was also called Manchester House and bears a tablet with the date and name. Thomas was one of the most able businessmen of the town, being involved with the management of the only bank, the 'Stourbridge and Kidderminster' which was on the site of the present Midland Bank. He lived in Monsieurs Hall. With Dipple, who had the ironmonger's just above him, he was owner of the new gas works just off the Worcester Road. They had a monopoly but the high prices they charged led to a public outcry, and soon after 1866, a public Gas Company was formed and the Thomas and Dipple monopoly ended.

The chemist's shop, one of three in High Street, belonging to Aaron Huxley was next to Thomas's. Huxley had a clever son who became a physician. Then there were two small shops, one of which belonged to a decorator and plumber, Mr. Rogers, who can be seen in the picture talking to Mr. Llewellyn Senior wearing a top hat and apron, whose grocer's shop is just behind him. Adjoining the passageway George Dipple kept a large ironmonger's. Besides being part owner of the Gas Works, he was a local celebrity, a churchwarden at St. John's, and involved in the management of the town. He fought for better roads round Bromsgrove and, in 1863, he threatened the Local Board with legal proceedings if they did not improve the road to Sidemoor and beyond. He described it as 'unsafe to pass over with any vehicle; it was narrower than the Act prescribed in many places, owing to recent enclosures'. He also complained about the deep ditches on each side as a danger to health, being little better than open sewers.

Beyond the entry was another chemist, Corbett Smith, and it was part of this that had been divided off to make the tiny Post Office. Above the chemist was the shop and house of Edward Perkins, an ironmonger and nailmaster. He and his family lived over their shop which probably was the imposing eighteenth century building still standing (no. 25). Edward Perkins was one of the wealthiest men in Bromsgrove and a great supporter of the Congregational Chapel in Windsor Street, now the United Reformed Church. After a small shop kept by Thomas Fisher, a saddler, came a good linen draper's shop owned by William Weaver. He too was a strong church supporter, attending the Catholic Chapel at Grafton Manor until the new Catholic Church was built at the bottom of Rock Hill in the 1860s. Another important coaching inn, the Star and Garter, was next kept by Henry Bullingham, but this was soon to close, another victim of the railway. Weaver's shop was probably the eighteenth century building still standing (nos. 33 and 35.)

A number of those in the engraving can be identified. In the middle foreground, with a walking stick, is Dr. Horton, and a second doctor, Dr. Haines, is on horseback talking to Scroxton, the bookseller. Yet a third doctor, Dr. T. S. Fletcher, can be seen with his small dog. Crossing the road are the vicar with his wife and daughter.

Dr. George Fletcher has dated the engravings to 1840 by means of the small dog in the picture which belonged to his father. George Fletcher's mother gave his father the dog soon after they were engaged and it died during the first year of their marriage. His father met his future wife, Miss Alcock, at the festivities for Queen Victoria's coronation in 1838 when tables were laid all down High Street from the Crescent to the Town Hall. Dr. Fletcher bumped against Miss Alcock carrying dishes out of the house of Mr. Robeson, a solicitor, which is now Lloyds Bank. Apologising to each other they were introduced then and there.

Bromsgrove's horse bus can be seen outside the Golden Cross Hotel taking on passengers for the new railway station. The 'railway bell' with its rope can be seen on the 'Cross' wall and this was pulled five minutes before the bus started. Likely lads often rang the bell and ran away. The horse had to travel up the dangerously steep Station Hill where coaches were sometimes overturned, and then along the lovely, winding country lane of Old Station Road to the railway. Apart from being the Tory party headquarters at election times as described on page 27, the Golden Cross was used for important meetings and dinners and political speeches were made from the hotel's balcony. It almost had a monopoly as a posting house, letting out carriages and broughams.

1852 saw an unusual event at the 'Cross' when it was host to the annual meeting of the Freemasons' Provincial Grand Lodge for Worcestershire.

Benjamin Maund and Thomas Housman were members of the Clive Lodge of Bromsgrove and had been appointed Provincial Grand Stewards. After the meeting at the 'Cross', the lodges formed a procession through the streets to the church where a masonic sermon was preached. The procession was led by the band of the Queen's Own Worcestershire Yeomanry Cavalry; the lodges carried their elegant but mysterious banners and guards marched with drawn swords. The hotel had a long association with freemasons as the earliest record of a lodge in Bromsgrove is St. John's. Its warrant is dated 11th July 1786 and it met at the Golden Cross.

Next above the Golden Cross was a house occupied by a teacher of music, Mr. Simms, who was organist at St. John's for forty years and whose son followed after him. Mr. Dell, a Quaker confectioner, had the rest of this building which is now Baylis's furniture store. Dell became a national figure in 1852 when his objection to militarism led him to refuse to put up his shutters, as the rest of Bromsgrove's shopkeepers had done, to observe the day of Wellington's funeral. Some of the older boys at Bromsgrove School seized him when next he was at the school to sell his wares and tossed him in a blanket in the school playground. He threatened to sue the school and was later paid about £60 in compensation. The school gained a lot of welcome publicity when a letter to *The Times* praised the patriotism of the boys, and there was a great increase in the number of boys wanting to enter the school.

After the wide yard entrance came a well known stationer and bookseller, J. H. Scroxton. He had a great shaggy head of hair, a kindly face, and heavy eyebrows and glasses and was one of the first of the town to take and sell photographs on glass. He tried to take a photograph of the young Queen at Bromsgrove station when the Royal train on its way to Birmingham was halted to take on the 'banker', used to push trains up the Lickey Incline. Unfortunately all he got in was a lot of smoke and the top of a first class carriage door. He brought out a monthly twopenny magazine called the Bromsgrove Gleaner which, according to Dr. Fletcher, was 'honest and peculiar and a little pedantic' like Scroxton himself. Several of the illustrations used in this book are his. He is remembered as one of the best and kindest of men.

The building next to the 'Cross' in the right foreground of the picture, and which is still standing, belonged to Joseph and William Greening. Joseph occupied a small farm, Red Cross in Perryfields Lane, and this assured the shop of a constant supply of fresh eggs and butter. His eldest son qualified as a surgeon and settled in the Isle of Wight.

Those shops in the lower part of the High Street which cannot be seen in the print started on the eastern side with Mrs. Frayne's – a large draper and haberdasher. It had 'London Frayne House' over the door. It was unusual for its day in that it had a plate glass window. Shops in London had started to install such large plate glass windows early in the century and this may explain the word 'London' in the shop sign. The boys from Bromsgrove School bought their straw hats from this shop, and their Cricket XI caps, blue for the first eleven and scarlet for the seconds. Another draper, Mr. Cordell was next, and then a small narrow shop that sold marbles, tops and slate pencils. Remarkably 130 years later, as Market Place Post Office, toys are still on offer there. The adjoining shop was a chemists. Mr. Haines, an apothecary, was as much an adviser as a chemist. People described their symptoms and he made up suitable remedies, saving many of the poor a doctor's fee. The brass plate on this very fine Victorian frontage, unaltered until 1989, reminded Bromsgrovians of the great respect the town had for Mr. Haines, apothecary and people's friend.

On the western side the first shop was a toy shop kept by a Mr. Fletcher and Morris's the tinsmiths was next door. It is now solicitors offices. Morris made kettles and saucepans in variety and made the best peashooters a boy could buy. Gillespy, who was a hairdresser next door, was also a musician who gave some excellent concerts in the town. He was also organist at Fernhill Heath and on cold wet Sundays could be seen driving a trap hired from the 'Cross' the nine miles to worship, costing him more in hire than his organist's small fee.

Other buildings which cannot be seen on the prints included a house (no. 52, currently used by the Nationwide Building Society) owned by a solicitor, Mr. B. H. Sanders, until he moved to the Steps House in St. John's Street, when it was taken over by Miss Knight for her Dame School. The site now occupied by new buildings, set back to accommodate a road widening scheme which has since been abandoned, was previously used by a number of properties. One of these was the Bell Inn, a good old fashioned place kept by Robert Harper, who did a thriving trade with the coaches which passed through the town. It was once called the Lower Dolphin and before that the White Swan. It was renamed the Bell by William Rose, the parish clerk and bell ringer when he became its proprietor. Next was Mr. Woodcock, a tailor, up four steps; an irascible man especially towards small boys. Then William Watton with a big butchers business, then a cooper's shop kept by Mr. Tudor and finally Mr. Wildsmith who sold second hand furniture, which brings us up to the new Boots chemist's store. The first part of this was another inn, the Green Dragon. Mr. Munslow kept it in the 1850s. He had a notice outside 'Pig market held here' and every Tuesday there was the squealing of pigs as they were driven up the yard. Friendly Societies had their annual dinners at the Bell or the Green Dragon on Whit Monday after they had marched to church behind a military band.

The shops between the Green Dragon and the Unicorn were a pawn broker's, a watchmaker's (Webley), a dealer in cheese and bacon (Watton), a small pork butcher's (Wall) and another shop kept by Moses Nokes. Mr. Watton was a very good cricketer who kept up the morale of his team by his good spirits. The Elizabethan timber framed building, now Rainscourts, was the Unicorn Inn, kept by Joseph Lacey, a tailor by trade, whose father kept the Shoulder of Mutton. The dignified Georgian style house which is now Lloyds Bank was occupied by a solicitor, Mr. Robeson, and later by his partner, Thomas Scott, who was a most efficient clerk to the magistrates, and a keen cricketer.

The house with perhaps the finest Georgian elevation, now Peacocks Stores, was owned by the Fletcher family in the 1850s. Dr. T. S. Fletcher and his brother Admiral Fletcher bought it in 1837. He was the first doctor in Bromsgrove to try out the new technique of using chloroform for operations. He had seen it demonstrated in Birmingham General Hospital in about 1850, and he returned to Bromsgrove bursting with delight at this new discovery of Dr. Simpson and telling all who would listen about it. Before the use of chloroform nearly half the patients having limbs amputated died. A surgeon needed at least two assistants to hold a patient down so violent were the poor victim's struggles. Despite this there was some opposition to its use, especially in childbirth, until Queen Victoria, to whom it was administered during the birth of Prince Leopold in 1853, referred to it as 'that blessed chloroform'. Dr. Fletcher obtained permission from Mr. Parkes at the Foxwalks Farm, down Grafton Lane, to try it out on a colt which needed an operation. He tied a towel well saturated with the stuff over the colt's nose but it remained as lively as ever. He then tried a nose bag filled with chaff and saturated with chloroform. The colt became unconscious and the vet performing the operation remarked, 'Why, Dr. Fletcher, it not only seems to be wonderful in stopping pain, but it partially stops the bleeding as well; you never told us that'. Dr. Fletcher replied, 'Oh no! the patient bled freely at Birmingham'. Then touching part of the tissues with a pair of forceps, he asked, 'What is this?' The vet looked carefully and Dr. Fletcher exclaimed, 'It is an artery; and the animal might well not bleed because he is dead!' This first trial was a disaster because he had not been told that a certain amount of air was necessary when using chloroform. Fortunately he took more lessons in its use before trying it out on his patients.

He was a particularly well loved doctor in the town because of his work in the 1849 cholera epidemic which swept the area. In Britain as a whole it killed 130,000 people. This terrible disease started with a 'prodigious evacuation, when the whole intestines seemed to be emptied at once, and it was followed by violent diarrhoea and vomiting in which the body lost several pints of fluid expelled as if from a syringe'. The doctor might find the bedclothes saturated and the floor of the bedroom awash. The loss of fluid from the body caused the skin and fingernails to turn blue or black and cause the patient to shrivel up to look more like a monkey than a man. Later the patient felt cramp as if he was being 'screwed through with a screw' until worn out, he would fall into a coma and die. Dr. Fletcher worked day and night to contain the outbreak and it was a common sight to see him, at all hours of the day and night, mounted on his raw-boned steed visiting his patients carrying a leather case with his instruments and medicine at the back of his saddle. The people of Bromsgrove and Stoke were so grateful to him for his work that they presented him with a silver tea and coffee service in Stoke schoolroom in 1850.

Most of the victims of cholera lived in the lower end of the town and at Stoke. The old cotton mill in Watt Close was used as a cholera hospital in the earlier epidemic of 1832. It was mainly spread by the excrement of patients getting into the water supply and the polluted brook carried the germs. It stank strongly in hot weather as it washed out and flowed under many of the closets in High Street, becoming even more polluted as it reached Worcester Street and Stoke. Most doctors believed wrongly that cholera was caused by poisoned air but Dr. Fletcher was early convinced that a supply of clean water was the answer. He pressed the Local Board to improve water supply and sanitation, but it was 1872 before the improvements he wanted were started.

In the 1850s most Bromsgrove people did not have a lavatory of their own. In Worcester Street where many nailers lived in terraces of houses, packed tightly together, a row of houses usually shared one outdoor earth closet. On the western side they were probably built to drain into the brook. Others were rarely emptied and most poor families relied on chamber pots which were emptied into the brook or onto any convenient waste ground. Middle class families had lavatories of their own but these were only unventilated cupboards which drained into the brook or into a cesspit which was liable to over-flow. Water closets were still a rarity in 1850; fewer than one house in twenty had one. Because the brook acted as a sewer the top end of the town was a good deal sweeter than the lower end.

Another doctor, Dr. George Horton, had a house built in 1857 just above the Fletchers and this three gabled Victorian, grey brick house still adds dignity to the upper end of High Street. There were two inns between this and the Stratford Road, the Coach and Horses and the Roebuck. Mr. Kenaz Keep of the Coach and Horses was one of the best known figures. In his ample yard he kept a variety of cabs and carriages for hire as well as a horse drawn omnibus which he ran three times a week to Birmingham. He always wore a long coat, a tall hat and a pleasant smile. It was a pleasure to travel with him for he never hurried his horses, never used his whip, preferring to urge them along with his voice. The Roebuck was an old coaching inn, a posting house for the mail coaches from London to Wolverhampton. It used to have a mounting block at its entrance.

On the other side of the street, next to the Crown was the only bank, the Stourbridge and Kidderminster, which is why the present Midland may well call it Old Bank House. It was managed by a Mr. Gibson and an appropriately named Mr. Penny lived on the premises. The very old building (no. 49) dating from the late seventeenth century next to the bank, was occupied by a dressmaker, then came Mr. Field, a draper and next door to him two spinster sisters, the Misses Blew. Mrs. Cook and her daughter at no. 55 did a lot of baking for Bromsgrove School and also let out rooms to masters there or to curates. The corner of Church Street was occupied by a private house rented by Dr. T. S. Fletcher between 1844 and 1861. Opposite to it, and just down Church Street, was the Cattle Market Tavern kept by William (alias Barber) Hill the town's bellman. He was a large man who could often be seen filling the doorway of his tavern, usually wearing a white apron with straps over his shoulders and a red waistcoat. He was known for his arresting advertisements one of which read, 'A quick shave and a glass of Bolding's Brilliant Bitter for 2d.' This tavern was formerly the old Sow and Pigs and before that Dunklin's Mug House.

There was a very small shop on the corner of High Street (no. 61) where Mrs. Kings made leather gloves and aprons and where later W. A. Cotton had his auctioneer's offices. Next was a fishmonger (Griffiths), then a cobbler (Penrice) and at no. 67, a Georgian building still standing, was a wealthy spinster Miss Mary Sanders. She had a very splendid funeral in the old style. Two 'mutes' were hired to stand on each side of the front door all the day of the funeral, each carrying a long black wand with a bunch of crepe tied at the top.

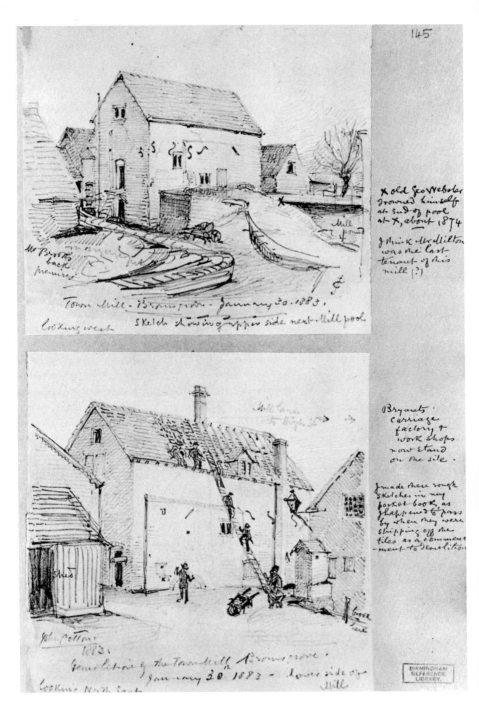

X old Geo Webster
drowned himself
at end of pool
at X, about 1874

J think Mr d Milton
was the last
tenant of this
mill (?)

Bryants
carriage
factory &
work shops
now stand
on the site.

J made these rough
sketches in my
pocket book, as
J happened to pass
by when they were
stripping off the
tiles as a commence
-ment to demolition

Town Mill - Bromsgrove - January 30. 1883.
Sketch showing upper side next Mill pool
Looking west

John Cotton
1883.
Demolition of the Town Mill Bromsgrove.
January 30th 1883 - lower side of Mill
Looking North East

John Cotton's sketches of the Town Mill.

Above Miss Sanders, Mrs. Green had young Dr. Prosser as a lodger. An assistant to Dr. Fletcher he was a flamboyant Tory supporter and at election times drove his gig up and down the street flaunting his Tory colours. On one occasion a mob assembled outside the house and threw stones through his window which provoked him to fire a pistol to disperse them. Dr. Joseph Horton, one of three brothers who were doctors, lived next door at the fine Georgian house which is now the Red Lion. His elder brother Thomas died in the cholera epidemic in 1849. After a wide yard the next building housed Mr. Dufill who had a string and rope shop; he had a rope walk at the back by the brook. Then came Seeley, a barber, then Troth, a coal middleman and William Hartle the blacksmith. He had a yard leading down to his forge and was the cricket team's demon fast bowler. Then there was another grocer, James Amiss and Martha Perkins, the widow of a nail factor who carried on his business.

Mill Lane led down to the Town Mill and at the top of the lane were William Brooke who sold seeds and flour and another double fronted flour and miller's shop kept by a Mr. Richmond. Rectory Manor, described earlier, was occupied in the 1850s by Joseph Milton who also owned Charford Mill. Next, up a few steps, was a clock-maker, Matthew Dodd. He once chased a burglar and caught him by his legs as he was escaping through a skylight. He got away by slipping out of his trousers, leaving them in Dodd's hands. Just above was the Mechanics' Institute, newly built in 1849, and it provided a reading room for workers in the town. This site is now the main Post Office. A Penny Bank was held in this Institute of which Dr. Collis, then headmaster of Bromsgrove School, was a Director. Every Tuesday he would ride his chestnut horse up to the Institute; both he and Mrs. Collis did a lot of riding and they also drove the last Irish jaunting car in Bromsgrove.

An old public house called the Dolphin was the last building but two on the western side of High Street; it was usually called the Upper Dolphin to distinguish it from the one later called the Bell but previously known as the Lower Dolphin. It was kept by Richard Gilbert and much used by workers at Jakeman's Tannery in pits and sheds alongside the Town Mill pool. In 1851 Gilbert was ordered to take down the old posts and chains in front of his inn; at that time there was a fine vine growing in front of it. Finally there was a family grocer's business owned by Thomas Wilson. J. B. Wilson bought the Upper Dolphin, the year after it was closed as an inn, in 1915.

Bromsgrove was still little more than one long street in the 1850s stretching from Rock Hill to the Crabmill, with open country on all sides. The population of the whole parish was only just over 10,000 and the parish covered a wide area. Footpaths led from the High Street to the countryside within minutes. There were few houses in Church Street, and St. John's Street was a quiet backwater, though there was a row of houses opposite St. John's steps. One of the loveliest walks led from Alcester Road (now Stratford Road) which was a country lane with a few cottages, across Mountfields to Ednall Lane, and then across Kiteless field, emerging in Charford by the mill. South Bromsgrove High School is now on the site of the mill and part of the mill pool has been retained. The line of this path is still preserved, though the old Kiteless Alley which ran from Ednall Lane through the Bromsgrove School grounds has been shifted to be a continuation of Conway Road. Footpaths from Ednall Lane, School Lane, Peters Finger, Martins Lane and Charford Lane led to Kiteless field in which the town's children were allowed to play freely. Most of these were closed and ancient rights of way lost in the twentieth century. From the Dragoon inn to the Worcester Road turnpike were only a few labourers' cottages and Charford mill. Broom House and Warwick Hall, both still standing, were the only two buildings passed by the horse bus on its way along the winding lane, Old Station Road, as it went to the station. Broom House is very ancient with its sandstone walls, mullioned windows and timber framing. Warwick Hall, a fine timber framed farm house, was occupied by Mr. Russon in the 1850s and he farmed the land around it as far as the eye could see. Leland's description of the area between Bromsgrove and Droitwich as 'having good corne, meetly wooded and well pastured' applied equally to all the land on either side of the town's one long street.

Nailmaking had replaced cloth making as Bromsgrove's staple industry in the eighteenth century. Most of the nailers lived in Worcester Street, in the Strand, up Stourbridge Road and in courts and lanes like Gas Square. They were noted for their hard drinking after long hours over a forge fire. This explains the many public houses in Worcester Street of which quite a few remain. D. C. Murray, the novelist son of a Black Country nailer, has given a graphic description of life in these surroundings. 'There was no hour in the twenty four when you could not hear the clink of the little hammer on the anvil. The nail workshop was fitted with a small forge and four or five little anvils. The children of our neighbours began almost in infancy. I have seen a girl of seven turning out her tale of wrought nails, six days out of seven that God sent, and boys were taught to use a hammer as soon as they could understand anything. The forge in the back kitchen was my earliest memory. I awoke permanently to a knowledge of the world whilst mother was working on the anvil. I was fixed in a sort of cloth bag upon her shoulders, and I remember peering round her neck at the glow of the fire, watching the iron rod as it became white-hot from the white-hot coke, and seeing her shape the end with dextrous blows into a nail, and then plunge the rod into the fire again. Father came in wet and bareheaded, carrying a ragged cap full of coke, which he had bought or borrowed from a neighbour. I can hear the tinkle of the hammer and its multiplied echoes from the cottages of our neighbours.'

One of the most familiar sights in Bromsgrove in the 1850s was the cheerful face of Jimmy Brown with his donkey and cart. He was a man of many parts, street hawker, ballad singer, dying speech man, and a rag and bone man. He hawked salt from Stoke Prior calling in a shrill voice, 'any rags, bones, rabbit skins or old iron. Any salt'. He often danced jigs in the street and his favourite expression was 'Dash my buttons', never using bad language. His first visit to Bromsgrove was as a dying speech man, singing and selling verses about the murder of Maria Martin in the Red Barn in 1828. He also sang verses about the transportation of Chartist leaders and prize fights. In Bromsgrove market he sang verses on the death of George IV and on the coronation and death of William IV and on Victoria's coronation. Attacking the Corn Laws, which kept the price of bread high, he sang: –

Says old John Bull here's a job
Shiver my timbers and break my knob,
The Waterloo Cock and Little Bob,
That carried the cursed Corn Bill,
They do set the nation in a blaze,
And kill the farmers with amaze;
They drive the landlords nearly mad,
And bye and bye they'll be so sad.

There never was such times
Since old Jonah swallowed a cod;
Cries old King George 'its a glorious job
To bury the cursed Corn Bill';
Flare up you British ladies all,
Tradesmen's wives, both great and small,
Shall have a petticoat, gown and shawl,
Made nicely out of the Corn Bill.

(the Waterloo Cock was the Duke of Wellington and Little Bob was Sir Robert Peel)

He first set up in Bromsgrove as a rag collector. He and his wife, with 'Coventry Bill', who wrote many of the ballads which Jimmy sang, lodged in a thatched cottage near the Black Cross kept by 'Old Beck Gordon'. Later he kept a lodging house previously kept by 'Joe Jew'; but he had to give it up because the rent of £10 a year proved to be too much for him. He then moved to a house next to Little Lane, taking in lodgers and selling crocks and collecting rags and bones. He did well with the rags, selling £35 worth every five weeks or so. His kindness to animals and children was well known, often buying buns for his donkey which took them from his mouth.

His love for children was best shown in his attendance at St. John's

Sunday School where he learned to read and write. After a time he instructed the children there in their alphabet, and when no longer needed as a teacher, joined the Young Men's Bible Class. For the Sunday School treat Jimmy decorated his donkey with evergreens and his cart was filled with children; a canopy overhead read 'Suffer little children to come unto Me'. This annual treat was often held at Breakback and, after tea, parents assembled in great numbers. Jimmy was at his best on Whit Monday when Bromsgrove was in its glory with the town's clubs and bands marching to church. He still attended Bible Class in his old age, but had to pay a small girl to carry his large printed bible because 'his breath would not let him get along'. When he died, aged 88, in 1888 his Bible Class companions carried out their promise to him and sang 'My God, My Father, while I stray' over his grave.

Jimmy Brown, like most Bromsgrovians who could read by 1850, had been taught to do so at Sunday School, or at the National School in Crown Close, apart from a small minority whose parents could afford to send them to private schools. These were the days before education was made compulsory by the 1870 Education Act. St. John's Sunday School was started in 1788 by William Brooke in a house opposite St. John's steps with two boys and seven girls. In 1833 the first purpose built school for children of less well off parents was opened and was called the National School because it received a grant of £200 from the National Society. The Sunday School also used the new building. A part of the profits of the town weighing machine had supported St. John's Sunday School since 1795 and £300 was raised by mortgage on the machine to help pay to build the new school. In 1846 the day school and Sunday School were united, supported by a common fund and managed by the same committee. In 1848 there were 186 children in the day schools and 867 in the several Sunday Schools of the town.

Discipline was much more severe then than now. When St. John's Sunday School was held in the Town Hall it was not unusual to see a boy being driven to it by his father wielding a big stick. A device known as a 'logger' was used at that time. It was a large round piece of wood, attached by a chain to the leg of a troublesome boy, who was obliged to hold the wood in his right hand. He had to walk to church with it and with his coat turned inside out, standing like this in front of the pulpit during the service. The birch was also used by the vicar to whip the bare back of a boy, whilst he was carried on the back of another boy up and down the schoolroom. A lad called Riley had the distinction of being the last boy to be punished in this way in 1836. Soon afterwards he was expelled from the school and later sentenced to be transported overseas.

Mr. Marcus, headmaster of the National School in the 1850s, believed in the maxim 'Spare the rod and spoil the child'. He often caned boys for trespassing on the grass of Crown Close which was rented by Mr. Haines of High Street for his cattle. The pupils had to keep to the small back yard. The classes were divided from each other by heavy curtains running on iron rods, and this caused a very oppressive atmosphere in hot weather. G. Bradfield, an old boy of the school, recalled in later years the strong anti-Catholic feeling, from which he, as a Catholic, suffered. He was continually taunted with cries of 'String the Pope'. John Humphreys was a pupil there too in the 1850s. He later became Professor of Dentistry at the University of Birmingham, a noted local historian, and Bailiff of Bromsgrove in 1895.

In the late 50s a town scandal was aroused over the primitive conditions in which the twelve 'Bluecoat' boys were taught at Bromsgrove School. Dr. T. S. Fletcher led the campaign to improve conditions for these 'Blue Chaws' as they had been called since Sir Thomas Cookes had re-endowed the school, stipulating that twelve poor boys of the town should be educated and clothed free of charge. These boys were set apart from the rest by their uniform and by being taught in a washroom, not being admitted to other school buildings. They wore long, thick, skirted, blue coats, leather belts, gaiters and peculiar mushroom shaped caps with large cloth buttons on top. They were taught by Mr. L. T. Saywell in an outhouse called 'Tosh House' by the other boys. It was next to the stables where four horses were housed and it had piles of manure just outside. This outhouse was used as a wash house by the smaller boys of the school after games and before meals. There were six jugs and basins kept in 'Tosh House' and a large barrel of water in the corridor, and the boys emptied the basins on the heaps of manure by the door. Though the basins were put in a corner when the 'Blue Chaws' came in at 9.30 a.m. for their lessons, they frequently found their seats were awash. They were only allowed to play in a large yard covered in ash pits where all the ashes from fireplaces in the rest of the school were emptied.

Dr. Fletcher, as a trustee for the foundation scholars, complained about these primitive conditions; but Dr. Collis, the headmaster, told him that he was well satisfied with the arrangements, 'considering the class of boy they are'. He said, 'The boys and their parents are content; the Oxford authorities at Worcester College holding the fellowships do not grumble, and as it appears a personal grievance for you and for the education of your sons, you had better let it rest'. It was not until Dr. Collis left in 1867 and Dr. Blore arrived that the arrangements were altered. A. E. Housman was awarded a scholarship under the new scheme in its first year, and so later were his four brothers.

A strong anti-Catholic feeling in Bromsgrove exploded when a new vicar, the Rev. C. H. Jenner, introduced High Church practices. He arrived soon after St. John's had been restored in 1859 and immediately abolished the old mixed choir reserving it for men and boys only. They were given white surplices to wear, intoning and chanting of prayers began, bowing the head at the name of Christ and standing up when the clergy entered the church, were introduced. The vicar's final step of preaching in a white surplice instead of the customary black gown triggered off a packed parish meeting in which loud protests were made about the Catholic flavour of the services. It was held in the Town Hall and was so rowdy that people outside could clearly hear the shouts of 'No Popery', 'Shut up' and 'Sit down'. One of the churchwardens, Thomas White, owner of the indigo factory (or 'Blue Works') in Watt Close, refused to listen to any more of the vicar's sermons and deliberately picked up his hat and books and walked out of the church down the centre aisle whenever Mr. Jenner made for the pulpit. White had strong support for his stand and, despite attempts to defeat him, he was re-elected as churchwarden. Incidentally the last traces of his 'Blue Works' only disappeared when a part that had been used as a Royal British Legion club was demolished in the 1970s to make way for a new squash club.

The class snobbery, so strong in Victorian Britain, was reflected in the views of a female member of St. John's as reported by Dr. George Fletcher. In an exchange of views about a new curate with a Low Church attitude, this lady replied 'Oh yes, Mrs. Fletcher, it is all very well to admire his preaching and his work. He is all very well for the afternoon service, for maidservants, shopgirls and children. He may do for them, but to save the souls of the chief of the congregation and of the upper classes, we must have the vicar.'

The sexton and clerk at St. John's was, at this time, Joseph Rose. The Rose family were a Bromsgrove institution, supplying clerks and sextons for five generations, beginning in 1772. Dr. Fletcher related one incident about Joseph Rose which involved an old burial custom. As a curious small boy he watched Joseph digging a grave and then saw him carry a little white wooden box about two feet in length from the church. He dug a small hole in the floor of the grave in which he placed the box, carefully covering it with earth. When young George asked what the box was for, Rose hesitated before replying, then he said that it contained a special sort of soil to hasten the decay of the coffin which would be placed above it. Later in life, Fletcher discovered he had witnessed the burial of a stillborn baby, carried out in that way to ensure the burial service was read over it. Joseph was appointed sexton in 1824 and continued in the post until 1868; he was the first member of his family to combine the offices of sexton and clerk from 1850, when his brother Will, who had been clerk for 31 years, died. Before the church restoration the clerk sat in the bottom of the old three-decker pulpit, a fine oak tub, with a sounding board and a dove on top. When a preacher of the 'hell fire' kind leaned over the front of the pulpit to indicate where most of the congregation would go, the fire passed harmlessly over old Will's head, as he sat underneath the parson, smiling like a portly cherub. The best view of Joseph Rose was as he tip-toed about the church in his slippers during a service, rapping the heads of sleeping worshippers with his long stick. Anyone just nodding off was given a gentle poke, but those who snored got a whack. The gentry were safe from his stick as they could sleep secretly in their higgledypiggledy high box pews. But the rest, who sat on open benches in their smock frocks and quaint bonnets, were very vulnerable to a poke from the sexton's stick.

In 1869 Joseph Rose's son, John, became sexton but ten years later he met with a terrible disaster. One March evening he climbed the belfry to wind up the church clock and, having done this and fastened the belfry window, he went towards the door in the dark and fell through the trapdoor in the floor 40 feet to the nave below. He died from his injuries. It is unlikely to be true, but a story has become part of the local folklore, that in trying to save himself he snatched at a bell rope and thus 'tolled his own knell'!

Living near the Rose family in St. John's Street was Sergeant Fawke, formerly of the Scots Greys. He fought in the Crimean War at Alma, Inkerman and Balaclava, returning home wounded. He became a professor of physical training and was a fine tall figure of a man; he demonstrated his skill as a swordsman at public entertainments where his tour de force was to cut through metal bars with one stroke of his sword.

Up a passage off Hanover Street lived two well known figures in adjoining cottages. Blind Soloman Wagstaff lived in the first cottage. He played the fiddle at local functions and made baskets and hampers for a living. Next door was Miss Mary Price, known as 'the Bible woman'. She was a teacher and superintendent of St. John's Sunday School for 48 years where her father had been superintendent before her. Mr. Price believed in the power of the cane and had used it vigorously and his daughter too had a reputation of having a wonderful way of keeping good order.

Whilst the Parish Church dominated one end of the town the new Union Workhouse dominated the other. These were the two largest buildings in the town: one to sustain the soul, the other the body. A numerous minority of Bromsgrovians were so desperately poor in the mid-nineteenth century that they were either forced to live in the workhouse or apply for payments from the Poor Rate, called 'outdoor relief'. These took the place of state unemployment pay, sick pay and old age pensions, none of which existed in those days. The poor were a perennial problem made worse by the number of vagrants passing through, especially along the Birmingham to Worcester Road. In 1862 there were 148 paupers in the new workhouse (it had a capacity for 350), and 862 people receiving outdoor relief; but these figures did not include vagrants.

Just as it dominated the town physically, the fear of having to enter the workhouse dominated the lives of the poorest Bromsgrovians. Only those facing starvation applied for admission because inmates were denied many basic human rights, and it was made very unpleasant for those who applied for outdoor relief. Immediately on entering the workhouse the inmates were labelled paupers and forced to wear distinctive clothing – suits of corduroy and black, flat round hats for the men; print dresses and starched bonnets for the women. Families were broken up, husbands being separated from their wives to prevent them breeding any more pauper children, and children were put in separate children's wards. They were put to work picking oakum, breaking stones and so on. Beds were straw mattresses and chaffbeds on iron bedsteads. Pauper children had to attend the pauper school; sick paupers were put in the pauper infirmary; and dead paupers were given pauper funerals. This final humiliation was a burial in the cheapest coffin with cord handles, costing eight shillings (40p), no lining and no shroud. The pauper body was taken on its final journey on a handcart pulled by four old men.

The mean treatment with which outdoor relief was granted was graphically described by County Councillor Joby Leadbetter when he became a member of the Bromsgrove Board of Guardians in 1894. Although he spoke of conditions as he knew them, they had been the same since the New Poor Law of 1834. He reported how a Bromsgrove woman who had applied for outdoor relief had been offered only 18 pence (8p) a week and was told she could take in washing to help her pay her way. Joby objected to the 'smallness' of this payment and pointed out to his colleagues on the Relief Committee that as her hands were covered with eczema sores she was unlikely to be a success as a washerwoman. What followed is best given in his own words: 'I was told to shut up and one member informed me that if I did not do so he would knock me through the window. I told two of the members that they would surely go to hell for their treatment of this poor soul, and that as chief officer of the town's fire brigade, it was no use them ringing me up to put out the fire as we should not turn out. A great storm arose and another member threatened to throw me over the staircase'.

In the 1890s Bromsgrove's workhouse wards for tramps were alleged to be the worst in the country at a time when 3 to 4000 men passed through them annually, mostly men who were searching for work. Leadbetter tested this allegation by disguising himself as a tramp and being admitted to the workhouse, where he found the washing arrangements appalling. He was forced to bath in the same water that six other tramps had used, when it resembled pea soup. There was but one towel available which all had to share. Most damaging of all, he observed, 'The poor man who took his bath before me unfortunately had running sores on his legs, and my feelings can be imagined'. Owing to protests such as those of Joby Leadbetter improvements were made in the last few years of the century.

The job of dealing with vagrants and arresting criminals and beggars was done by two men, mainly, until 1840. They were Jimmy Kings, the Runner, and Thomas Edwards, the Nightwatchman and Town Crier. The gaol, which was demolished in the 1890s, was in the Strand behind the old workhouse, still standing at the top of the High Street. It consisted of four cells and had two storeys with a thatched roof and a door, heavily studded with iron. Kings was a terror to all lawbreakers because of the speed and energy with which he pursued them across country. In 1840 he became the first Superintendent of Police when the County Police Force was formed. A new Police Station and Magistrates Court was built in Station Street; it is now used as a factory. It was vacated by the police when the new Police Station was built in 1890. When Jimmy Kings finished his daytime duty Thomas Edwards took over as nightwatchman. He was that for eleven years and town crier for forty seven, from 1827 to 1874. He had a remarkably deep and powerful voice and a few pints of ale helped him get through his announcements. He was crier, ale and bread-taster to the Court Leet and Baron. For years he sang an anti-Catholic and anti-Stuart song at the Court Leet dinner called 'Church and State and no surrender'. On duty he wore a great coat and broad brimmed hat and carried a lantern, rattle and staff. He called out the time every half hour and the state of the weather at the end of his beat. For example 'Half past five and a cold frosty morning'. He was powerfully built and few criminals chose to argue with him. At one time he taught at St. John's Sunday School, but Captain Adams of Perry Hall advised him to give it up as he often overslept, having only come off duty at 5 a.m. on the Sunday morning. A leading member of the Oddfellows Order, a Provincial Grand Master, he often walked to Oddfellows' meetings at Droitwich and Belbroughton.

Reports from the Bromsgrove Messenger of 1860 show that superstition and folklore were still rife. One story current at that time, which many local people seemed to believe, concerned a farmer who had prayed that he might be sent to sleep until the rainy season was over, because of the damage already done to his crops. Directly after this impious prayer he had fallen into a trance on the spot and it had proved impossible to move him. In the reporter's own words 'His arms hung down by his side, his eyes were nearly closed, his breathing was imperceptible, but his pulse continued to beat though faintly; his head hung a little on one side and his mouth was partially open. His friends pushed him, but they found him rooted to the ground as a tree; they fetched a team of seven horses, harnessed them with ropes, and attempted to pull him along, but they could not move him an inch. Burnt feathers, snuff, hartshorne, and mustard could promote no sign of consciousness'. An iron shed was then built over him to protect him from the weather. The exact location of this unfortunate farmer varied in the story, but a group of rustics from outside the area had arrived in the town during the week ending 1st September and had gone straight to Crown Close where they had heard the farmer was rooted.

Another report, dated 13th October 1860, is about a commotion in the High Street, where this account of Bromsgrove begins and ends, and is a reminder of how rural the town still was. It is about a vicious cow who butted the hindquarters of a horse on which sat a Mr. Jones as he talked to Mr. Hartle outside his butcher's shop one evening. The painful shock to its rump caused the horse to rear and jump over Mr. Hartle who had fallen down in the confusion. The cow continued on its headlong career and, at the corner of Hanover Street, attacked a Mr. Milward, who had tried to stop it, knocked him down and left him senseless. It then dashed down Worcester Road at a fearful pace and, after knocking an old man called Tustin against a wall, was finally turned at the Rock Hill turnpike by some men returning from Stoke Works. They drove the cow in the direction of Charford and so on towards home.

Chapter Three

Grafton Manor

by John Weston

The Manor showing on the right of the picture the 1567 wing which survived the great fire of 1710.

3

Just a mile south of Bromsgrove and down a beautiful lane leading from the main road lies Grafton Manor. This attractive old house was for 700 years the home of two of the most powerful families in English history – the Staffords and the Talbots. Its importance was such that Camden described Bromsgrove as "a mercate town not of the meanest reckoning" and "not farre from Grafton". In fact Grafton has always been an important place since it first fell to Urso d'Abitot, cousin of the Norman conqueror, after the Battle of Hastings. Subsequently, it passed into the hands of the Graftons who held it from the time of Henry I to Edward I, then to the Hastings, a Warwickshire family, until about the middle of the 13th century whence it passed by marriage to the Staffords. In 1450 Sir Humphrey Stafford was Lord of Grafton, a soldier of high reputation and in constant attendance upon King Henry VI. He met his death in one of the most striking events of that time, Jack Cade's rebellion and his body was brought home to be buried in the parish church at Bromsgrove. His wife erected to his memory the magnificent stone-tomb which can be seen and admired to this day.

Thirty-five years passed, made eventful by the Wars of the Roses until in 1485 Henry Tudor landed at Milford Haven and was hailed as the saviour of his country. He quickly gathered together a force of 5000 men including a large contingent led by Sir Gilbert Talbot, High Sheriff of Shropshire. Worcestershire's High Sheriff at that time was Sir Humphrey Stafford of Grafton, nephew of the ill-fated Sir Humphrey of Jack Cade's rebellion. He joined the Royal Army of Richard III and the two forces met at Bosworth Field. Henry Tudor's army was outnumbered by two to one but what they lacked in numbers they made up for in bravery and spirit and all had a single aim, to rid the country of Richard, whose infamous deeds had made his name detested. Sir Gilbert Talbot led the vital right wing of Henry's attack and so well did they fight that the Royal Army retreated, Richard was slain and the fight became a rout. Sir Humphrey Stafford and some others escaped but later they were found and Stafford paid the penalty at Tyburn. His vast estates were given by the grateful monarch to Sir Gilbert Talbot, the hero of Bosworth Field, and from then on he took up residence at Grafton Manor.

Sir Gilbert Talbot was an imposing personality and Henry loaded him with honours and large estates. He became a Knight of the Garter and later Governor of Calais, the most important post held by a subject outside England. Henry granted to him, and his male heirs, the Manor of Grafton which was held by the family until 1935. They were also granted much land in other parts of Worcestershire all forfeited by the Staffords. He was given many diplomatic missions to perform on behalf of the King and in 1503 was sent with the Abbot of Glastonbury to congratulate Pope Pius III on his election to the Papacy. Sir Gilbert was twice married, his first wife, Elizabeth, died only 4 years after they came to Grafton and lies buried in St. John's Church in a magnificent alabaster tomb.

John, the grandson of Sir Gilbert, succeeded in 1555 and in 1567 he rebuilt Grafton on a grand scale. It is fortunate that many details of this rebuilding were revealed by the discovery of the Elizabethan Estate Book of Grafton Manor which covers the period from 17th November, 1568 to 31st October, 1569. Some idea of the great extent of the mansion can be gleaned from the building that is there today though a fire in 1710 did very great damage. The park which surrounded the house covered some 420 acres and many of the nearby farms still bear names which indicate its limits: East Lodge, West Lodge, Park Gate, Warridge Lodge, etc. The gardens were laid out in terraced slopes leading down to the pool and enclosed in brick walls all of which remains today, an accurate representation of an Elizabethan garden.

Fish was a necessity for fast days in this large Catholic house and these were obtained from the lake and from fish stews which were built in the garden to hold fish fed up and ready for the table.

Though the fire of 1710 destroyed the greater part of John Talbot's splendid home, the porch, entrance-hall and the gable to the right of it survived and indicate the beautiful proportions of the whole. Above the porch are the arms of Queen Elizabeth I with the date 1567 and over a nearby window is inscribed:

> "Plenti and grase
> Bi in this place
> Whyle every man is pleased in his degree
> There is both peace and unity
> Salaman saith there's none accorde
> When every man would be a lorde"

A fine Tudor Barn said to have been used by Cromwell adjoins the Manor House together with a lovely little chapel and a priests house. There must have been a chapel on the site before 1218 for in that year the tithes of Grafton Chapel were assigned to the upkeep of the lighted candles round the tomb of King John in Worcester Cathedral. Here also was a round dovecote (still standing), dungeons and a spacious lake with an attractive island. The lake is remembered by older Bromsgrovians as a popular place for skating when the ice bore.

John Talbot was probably the wealthiest landowner in Worcestershire at this time and appears to have lived mainly at Grafton, though he had a mansion at Pepperhill, near Albrighton, Shropshire. But he lived in troubled times for as a Roman Catholic he paid a high price for his principles. Those who would not attend Church were subject to ruinous fines and John Talbot certainly paid out a small fortune together with several other leading families in the area. Among these were the Lyttletons of Hagley, the Windsors of Hewell, the Habingtons of Hindlip and the Wyntours of Huddington, all of whom clung to the old religion despite the risks they ran by so doing. Catholics were ordered not to go more than 5 miles from home and to harbour a priest was high treason. The oppressed Catholics felt bitter that freedom of worship was denied them and feelings ran so high amongst some of the younger spirits that a wild scheme was thought up with disastrous results. It was The Gunpowder Plot of 1605.

John Talbot's son in law was Robert Wyntour of Huddington Court, near Droitwich and it was at this house that many details of the Plot were agreed. It is also known that on Sunday, 3rd November Robert Wyntour spent the day at Grafton before riding to Dunchurch to join the other conspirators and await news of the mad enterprise. There is no evidence that John Talbot, then 64, knew of the Plot or had any hand in it despite the involvement of so many of his friends and relatives. He in fact was at Pepperhill, his Shropshire home, when on the Wednesday evening a horseman galloped furiously up to the house with a dramatic tale. It was his cousin who brought news of the plot, its failure and the plight of his son in law now labelled a traitor. By the next night the exhausted plotters, fleeing for their lives had reached Holbeach, 10 miles from Pepperhill, and in their desperate state asked Robert Wyntour to go on ahead and seek refuge from his father in law. Robert refused to implicate anyone else, but his brother and Stephen Lyttleton agreed to try and reached the house on Friday morning. John Talbot would have none of it and turned them away reproaching them for seeking to involve him as an innocent victim.

The two returned to Holbeach and soon afterwards the house was surrounded by the Sheriff's forces and the conspirators all killed or captured. The Wyntour brothers were later executed and although John Talbot remained under suspicion for some considerable time he was later cleared.

Grafton Manor was chosen at about this time to be the chief mission centre in East Worcestershire. There were many such centres where the local Catholics held a secret Mass usually in an upper room. One such, preserved to this day and open to visitors, being Harvington Hall, near Chaddesley Corbett which is an outstanding example of its type. It has many ingenious hiding places where a priest could be secreted and remain hidden while soldiers searched within inches of him. There can be little doubt that Grafton had similar places though unlike Harvington these have been lost due to the fire and the passage of time. Though, as has been said earlier, there is no evidence to support the legend of a tunnel from the Manor to the Shoulder of Mutton, or the Parish Church, it is possible that, like Harvington, a tunnel of some 200 yards may have been available to enable a priest to escape when he found the house surrounded. Father Oldcorne had charge of the Grafton mission in 1605 but was captured at Hindlip Hall and executed later for concealing one of the conspirators. He had been conducting services in the homes of the local Catholic gentry for 20 years while ministering to his scattered flock.

The mission at Grafton continued without a break for three centuries until in 1860 the chapel next to the Manor was closed for public worship and was replaced by the present St. Peters Church at the bottom of Rock Hill. Helen Wyntour, daughter of the Gunpowder Plot Conspirator made a most beautiful set of vestments for the use of the Grafton priest which were kept there until 1854 when they were transferred to Stonyhurst, the well-known Lancashire Catholic Boys School. There is little doubt that these vestments were used by Father John Wall, the Jesuit priest during his long mission in the area.

Father Wall whose headquarters were at Grafton, was also chaplain to Lady Yate of Harvington Hall. After the Titus Oates Plot of 1678 when all Jesuits came under suspicion, Father Wall was caught by unlucky chance at Rushock Court, about a mile from Harvington. He was arrested and after a long trial was hanged on 22nd August, 1679, being the last man to die for his faith in Worcestershire. Two hundred years later a stone monument was erected to his memory in the little churchyard at Harvington. Every year on the anniversary of his death, hundreds of pilgrims of all shades of religious opinion meet at this spot to honour a good man and a devoted servant of God.

It has been written about the Talbots of Grafton that "No family in England is more connected with the history of our country than this noble race; few are more highly allied." The old manor house must have seen a wealth of interesting events over the centuries being closely associated with so many of the important happenings of the time. Grafton remained in Talbot hands until 1934 when it was sold to Alfred Murray-Willis. It became a rest home for the elderly in 1946 but in the 1980s much of the house was restored to its former glories and opened as a high class restaurant. The Talbot coat of arms can still be seen in the Great Parlour, a most splendid room and one of the few that survived the fire. John and June Morris and their family who carried out the restoration deserve much credit for their work in undertaking a daunting project. Grafton remains as a gracious monument to some of the most enthralling chapters in the turbulent history of England.

Chapter Four

St. John's Church

by Robert Pancheri

St. John's Church from the North East.
From an engraving in the Cotton Collection.

4

It would be idle to speculate for how long the steep little hill in Bromsgrove has been in use as a seat of worship; but certainly one stone cross and two effigies found in the graveyard seem to be older than any part of the present church. These three objects are now grouped together in a recess in the south wall as a memorial to a former vicar, F. G. Shepherd. They are also, by implication, a memorial to another, Maurice Dean, whose idea it was to place these relics there, and who also found in a near-by garden, and begged for the church, that little cube of stone which he recognised to be the heart burial of a knight who had been killed in the Third Crusade – and this too takes us back to the earliest period of the building of the church at the end of the twelfth century.

The only recognisable work we have of this period are the two piers of the south door which, as the arch is of a later date, would seem to have been rebuilt and one might think it originally formed part of a south wall on the line of the fifteenth century arcade. Bromsgrove people owe some debt of gratitude to Sir Gilbert Scott who restored the building in the nineteenth century, removing the eighteenth century plaster, in that he replaced all the details, where evidence existed, faithfully as he found them. In consequence we have the print of the twelfth century string course and piers in the area of the pulpit, and in the capitals of the thirteenth century arcade, in which he did not miss the subtle variations in the mouldings to the capitals, and preserved it all for us. The weak little masks which serve here and at the chancel arch as drip-stone terminals are the work of one, Naylor, whose work can be recognised in all the churches and many of the nineteenth century buildings in Bromsgrove.

An adequate guide book is usually available in the church dealing with its architecture and monuments. It is intended here to tell of the connections the church has had with important personalities and historical events during its long existence. As a basis, and disregarding chronological sequence, let us start with Alan Hinksman and his memorial. He was the son of a vicar of Dodford and distinguished himself in the field of electrical engineering, making a significant contribution to the defence of the nation during the Second World War as a clever inventor. In 1940 the Germans had begun to drop magnetic mines in the estuary of the Thames which could be detonated by ships passing over them. To counter this device Barnes Wallis, the inventor of the 'bouncing Bomb' used to destroy the German dams, enlisted Hinksman's services to design and make some huge electromagnets to be slung under Wellington bombers which would sweep over the water and cause the bombs to explode harmlessly. Later in the war he specialised in under-water listening technology. He was always a regular church goer and for many years turned up at 7.45 on Sunday mornings to toll the bell for early communion. He was deeply interested in Bromsgrove history, a keen member of the Court Leet, and its Bailiff in 1968. When he died the next year his family commissioned an organ screen in St. John's Church as a memorial to him and it was thought that some reference to his abiding interest would be an appropriate basis for its theme. This shall now serve as a matrix for a tale of Bromsgrove's Parish Church.

The screen was designed with ten bays, each with its own little contribution to the story. In the first bay, by way of introduction, John the Baptist is seen giving advice, as in St. Luke's Gospel, to the tax gatherers and the Roman soldiers. Speaking thus from the heart of the church to the secular world he might be regarded as a link between the gospel story and established history. In the second bay his namesake, King John, who gave Bromsgrove its charter and fair, is seen. He is depicted as on his tomb at Worcester Cathedral with the fateful seal in his hand and it is set against the opening sentence of Magna Carta.

In the third bay Sir Humphrey Stafford of Grafton Manor is being dragged by his feet behind Jack Cade's horse through the streets of London and William Shakespeare is writing his play about it, King Henry VI part II. It is not known whether Jack Cade actually did this to Sir Humphrey after he had killed him, or only said he would do it; but certainly he killed him and Lady Alianora went to London to claim his body and brought it back to be buried in the church; and the splendid tomb is to be seen there still. As is told in the chapter on Grafton Manor, Bromsgrove had many connections with the Gunpowder Plot – the conspirators holed up at Hewell Grange and at Hagley Hall – but the closest one lies in the fact that Robert Wintour's wife was a daughter of John Talbot of Grafton Manor. It was at her house, Huddington Court, that her husband, two brothers, their cousin John Catesby and some others, after supper on Christmas Eve 1604 took a solemn vow to 'blow up the King in Parliament'. In the fourth bay therefore may be seen Guy Fawkes with his twelve barrels of gunpowder in the Palace of Westminster, with James I in effigy above.

After his defeat at the battle of Worcester, Charles Stuart escaped north to the village of Tong near Albrighton where, so as not to implicate his hosts at Boscobel Farm in his escape, he hid in the famous oak tree. To get away from there he disguised himself as a serving man, taking the name of William Jackson, and travelling south with a Mistress Jane Lane, who had a pass to visit her sister at Bristol who was expecting a baby. On the way they passed through Bromsgrove and as their horse cast a shoe coming over the Lickey Hills they stopped – some say at the Black Cross – to engage the services of a farrier. Legend has it that as Charles watched him putting on the shoe he said he wished he could 'catch that Charles Stuart and claim the reward'. Charles and Jane can be seen in the fifth panel riding their strawberry roan horse beneath a crown that is still to be won and against a background of oak leaves.

The sixth bay shows Sir Thomas Cookes of Norgrove Court, Bentley. It is told that he had a wager with a friend about who had the better butler. To settle this they agreed that each should give a banquet at which the butlers would serve and they would then ask the guests to decide the issue. Cookes gave the first banquet and, when all the guests were assembled at the table and ready to start the meal, he asked his friend if all was in order. After a survey of the table the friend remarked that there was no spoon for the salt. In a fit of rage Cookes plunged a knife into the stomach of the unfortunate butler. For this crime he was sent to prison and, when he came out, as penance he re-endowed Bromsgrove School, granting twelve foundation scholarships and requiring that every year the trustees '...Shall nominate or appoynt some Learned Minister to read Prayers and preach a sermon in the church at Bromsgrove on the first day of May.' Icely, in his book 'Bromsgrove School through Four Centuries', says that no evidence can be found to substantiate this strange tale. 'On the other hand' he says, 'the love for his wife manifest in the fine monument to the Lady Mary Cookes in Tardebigge Church, his friendship with Bishop Lloyd of Worcester, and his loyalty to Church and King, all point the other way.' But it is a good story and shown in the carving, which is based on Kneller's portrait of Sir Thomas, he is seen holding the fatal carving knife in his hand. His crest, his shield and his motto which he gave to the school are also shown.

Bromsgrove's connection with Admiral Byng might be considered tenuous, but when the screen was made Miss Byng who could trace her ancestry to the unhappy Admiral had been principal of the Sunday School of St. John's Church for some forty years and her brother, a well known local florist, had decked parish funerals for a generation. So Admiral Byng is shown on the deck of the Monarque being shot for failing to relieve the garrison of Minorca – which prompted the French satirist to observe that in England it is necessary to shoot an admiral from time to time 'in order to encourage the others'. This immortal aphorism is carved on a ribbon in the rigging.

The eighth panel shows Alfred Housman writing poetry in his favourite tree at Perry Hall beneath the church tower. The ninth has a reference to the Gates of Buckingham Palace made here in Bromsgrove, with one of the famous Weingartner keyholes. More about this, of course, in the chapter on the Guild. The last bay reflects the sentiment of the first. John the Baptist has given all that splendid advice to the secular world, and here Salome tells him what the secular world will do with it. She has his head on a meat dish, effectively silenced, while his body lies lifeless on the dungeon floor.*

Situated on the south wall of the church is the Royal Coat of Arms which is an object of local interest. This was a device introduced in 1801 to mark the Act of Union with Ireland in 1799, though the harp of Ireland had been included on the third quarter by James I ninety years earlier. The alteration which was made to this Coat was the removal of the shield of Hanover from the fourth quarter, to make way for a second shield of England, and placing it instead on a little shield of its own in the centre. Superimposed on this shield again is the escutcheon of the Crown of Charlemagne, with its six little gold plates clipped round the Sacred Nail. In those times heraldic draughtsmanship rejoiced in comic vulgarity, reflecting perhaps the cynical disrespect people had for the Prince Regent. This was evidently the attitude of the local signpainter who produced this work. When he came to the Crown of Charlemagne he showed the Nail, not beaten circular as it was, but cocked up gaily out of the side like a feather in a lady's hat. And it was not the sort of nail that the Romans used in crucifixions but the sort of nail that was being made in Bromsgrove at that time. Queen Victoria, of course, was not amused by such frivolity and one of her first acts was to abolish the shield of Hanover in its entirety and to introduce the Royal Coat of Arms as we have it today.

The furnishing of the Lady Chapel sheds an interesting, if feeble, light

---

* This screen was carved by Robert Pancheri, author of this chapter. (ed.)

on the liturgical vicissitudes of the seventeenth century. It was designed in the early part of the twentieth century by Sir Reginald Blomfield, who may have been introduced to the job by Walter Gilbert, whose story is told in the chapter on the Guild. It was sited at the east end of the south aisle, where the organ is now. It is now behind the Stafford Chantry facing north, a position to which it was moved in 1946. Blomfield used as an altar an oak table with four turned legs which had evidently been brought into the church in the seventeenth century. As it was the express decree of Archbishop Laud that all tables should have their two back legs flat so that they could be nailed to the east wall, one wonders if, perhaps, Bromsgrove defied his decree; in the matter of ritual St. John's has had a long tradition of low-churchmanship. To form a reredos to his altar Blomfield used an odd bit of eighteenth century panelling into which he inserted a panel of the seventeenth century carving of the Last Supper, which is one of the most interesting objects in the church. The classical riddel posts are his design, but the Gothic glazed screen between that and the choir was designed by Allen of Bromsgrove Guild.

The Vicars' Board was made by the Guild in its earlier period and, like all vicars' boards, is a record of immense interest. One name worth particular note is that of Francis Pagett, who was sent to Bromsgrove for two years to gain parochial experience before going on to become Bishop of Oxford. In that capacity he had the dubious distinction of refusing ordination to William Temple, who was later ordained by someone else, and went on to become one of the best loved Archbishops of Canterbury. In his autobiography Pagett tells of the grinding poverty in the parish due to the decline of the nailing industry, and of his efforts to promote the sale of nails. He had some little boxes made up containing a hammer and assorted nails which he hoped people might give to one another. It is hardly necessary to say that this impractical ploy met with no success and his parishioners had to resign themselves to their misery.

Together with the other stories told in this book this may serve to remind us that the lofty walls of St. John's have stood in 'midst of other woe than ours'. Yet still we pray, if we may borrow another line from Keats, that they might 'keep a bower quiet for us, and a sleep full of sweet dreams, and health, and quiet breathing.'

Chapter Five

The Watermills of Bromsgrove

by Jonathan Briggs

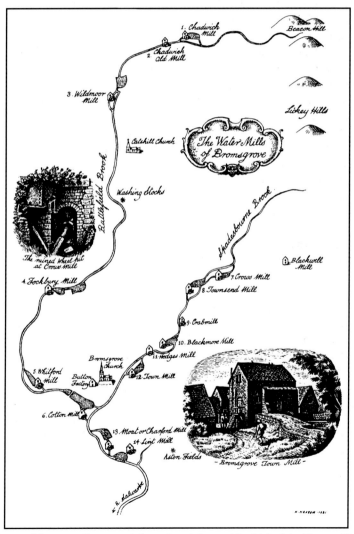

This map of the watermills was specially made and decorated for this book by Norman Neasom A.R.S.W.

5

The two brooks of Bromsgrove, the Spadesbourne and Battlefield Brook join at the lower end of Sanders Park. In former times the waters of these two streams powered many mills and factories. Numerous industries were served, including some long forgotten in Bromsgrove, such as textile mills, and the needle and fish hook factories. By the middle of the nineteenth century these industries had died out in the town. There were, in addition to these less usual industries, the corn and saw mills more commonly associated with water power.

In order to maintain a regular supply of water each mill had a millpool or a complex of pools. Bromsgrove must have been very different then; in the town centre there was a large pool where the Mill Lane Precinct is; in the area of Sanders Park was the Cotton Pool covering six or seven acres; and at the corner of the Charford and Worcester Roads there was a complex of pools to power the Moat Mill and the Lint Mill. Besides the millpools there were often large additional storage pools, such as those at Fockbury and Wildmoor, long since dry.

Without the pools it is difficult to imagine that the two streams carried so much potential power. But even with the normally deep millpools there were occasions when the water got low. In the hot summer of 1863 the millers took the liberty of poaching water from farmers' irrigation channels resulting in serious loss of crops. Millpools were also often the scene of suicides and of accidental drownings.

Corn mills were the longest lasting and commonest watermills in Bromsgrove, nearly all of those recorded having been used for corn grinding at some time. In its broadest sense the term 'corn grinding' covers the processing of cereals in general and can include flour, grist, chaff-milling, batch-grinding and sharps-grinding both for human consumption and for stock feed. All these processes would have been carried out in Bromsgrove's corn mills. The needle and fish hook industry was based at Stoke Prior in the Needle Mill and Fish House Mill. This industry declined in Bromsgrove in the early nineteenth century, whilst at

Redditch it flourished. In addition to these activities Bromsgrove was once a well known and important centre for textile manufacture. Elizabeth I granted a licence to Bromsgrove for the manufacture of cloth; wool and linen were the textiles made. The production of the raw materials was an important part of farming in the district and the blue flowered fields of flax must have been a beautiful sight. The poem which starts chapter two reflects the importance of this trade. Bleaching grounds, nogging shops and other stages in the textile manufacturing process, perhaps based in smaller buildings, were in the Sidemoor, Cherry Orchard and Hanover Street areas, but the major part of the textile process took place in the watermills. The best examples of these were the Cotton Mill and the Lint Mill, which was once a worsted mill.

The reason most commonly given for the decline of these industries is that no-one in Bromsgrove had the enterprise or capital to improve his establishment. Whether or not this is true linen manufacture was last carried out by a Mr. Haines in the 1840s, though the Lint Mill continued production until the middle of the twentieth century. The woollen industry survived until the 1880s in the form of wool-stapling under a Mr. Harrison at the Cotton Mill. In the latter half of the nineteenth century there was a marked increase in the number of corn mills adapted to include saw-milling. This may be a reflection on the demise of the textile industry or evidence of an increased demand for sawn timber. Another reason may have been the increase in number of large, steam powered, flour mills. The most important of these were a Mr. Finney's Aston Fields Flour Mills and Stoke Prior Flour Mills (once water powered). Both establishments were very large and valuable and both were destroyed by fire; in 1888 and 1896 respectively. Among the corn mills which advertised sawing facilities were Fockbury, Town, Moat and Blackmore Mills.

The rapid succession of millers at Bromsgrove's corn mills is remarkable. Apart from Townsend Mill all the mills seem to undergo a tenancy change every few years. Often these changes were due to the migration of a miller from one mill to another. By the beginning of the twentieth century most of Bromsgrove's water powered corn mills were suffering from the competition of steam mills. Few survived beyond about 1920 with the notable exception of Townsend Mill which, under Jabez Bridgman continued to grind using water power until about 1950.

The following section numbers refer to the decorative map of Bromsgrove's mills used as a title page to this chapter.

BATTLEFIELD BROOK

1. 2. & 3. The Wildmoor Mills

There were three mill sites in Wildmoor. Wildmoor Mill itself on Mill Lane, Chadwich Mill, and an unnamed mill on Wildmoor Lane. Little is known about any of these mills. Wildmoor Mill, now part of a farm, was in the Allsebrook family from the 1860s to the end of the nineteenth century and in use until 1912, when Frank Pearman was the miller. Chadwich Mill, like Wildmoor, was a farm mill – run by and for the farmer. It stands apart from the Chadwich Farm and has been converted to a house.

4. Fockbury Mill

During the latter half of the nineteenth century Fockbury was a corn mill run by the Ince family and owned by William Stableford. A solicitor, John Rotton, bought the premises in 1896. William Ince advertised himself as a steam and saw miller in 1873, but corn was still ground by water power into the twentieth century. In 1926 the mill and farm house became the property of the Crawford family. Though the mill building stands, it is isolated from the brook by the M5 motorway and the mill pool has been filled in.

5. Whitford Mill

This mill stood at the corner of Timberhonger Lane until about 1936. It was a farm mill standing adjacent to Whitford Farm until the latter was rebuilt on a new site in the 1900s. Mr. Lammas was the last miller and farmer and when the housing estate was built on the farmland in the 1970s he stayed in the farm house. He used the mill for oat and chaff milling, but before this it was a flour mill under a succession of millers. J. and E. Brewster (1820), T. Harrison and W. Pearsall (1838), Isaiah Godfrey (1840), John Worsey (1860 to 1880), Evan Watkin (1880) and W. H. Overton (1884 to 1893) are a few of the occupiers. A bungalow stands on the site of the mill.

6. Cotton Mill or Buck House

This mill standing at the end of Watt (or Water) Close and Factory Lane was amongst those licensed for cloth manufacture by Elizabeth I. It was remarkable for its huge mill pond – the Cotton Pool – which covered six or seven acres of what is now Sanders Park. In winter months this pool provided local people with an open air ice-skating rink. It was also a great favourite with fishermen. Great numbers of fish were stranded when the pool was drained in July 1865. The mill building was also substantial, long, narrow, and four and five storeys high. As the textile industry declined it was put to other uses. Thus in 1831 it became the Boys Sunday School and in 1832 it served as a cholera hospital.

James Sanders bought the mill as a 'disused spinning mill' from John Knight in 1853 and let it as a worsted factory to Messrs Adams. By 1856, however, it was again disused. A Mr. Harrison rented the building for woolstapling, as was mentioned in the introduction to this chapter, though by 1890 this use too was finished and in 1892 Mr. Benjamin Sanders pulled it down. Some of the bricks from the mill walls were used to construct the model cottages nearby. Mr. Sanders made an open air swimming bath on the site where many townspeople learnt to swim until a modern, indoor and heated pool was built in School Drive after the Second World War.

The Sanders family were more successful at the Button Factory, which itself had once been a cotton mill, which they bought in 1810. Their patent for making cloth covered buttons provided much needed employment for women. One hundred and seventy years later the business was still flourishing making metal badges under the Nicholls family who first came as managers for the Sanders and then took over as the Sanders male line died out. It was a Sander's will that gave the town its Park of that name. Many of the members of the clan lived in the best houses in and near the town. One, a solicitor, was clerk to the local authority for over fifty years in the nineteenth century and early part of the twentieth century. A horse trough which used to stand at the top of the town at the junction of Stourbridge and Birmingham Roads was erected to his memory; appropriately it was moved to Sanders Park.

THE SPADESBOURNE
7. Crows Mill

Crows Mill at Lickey End is derelict as a mill but retains some machinery. Every angle of view shows its picturesque setting with the mill pool on one side and the thatched, half timbered cottage on the other. The site is very ancient on the line of the old Roman Road, a continuation of High Street, running under its garden. It was last used as a grist mill in 1917 by the Dodwell family. They had been at the mill and farm for sixty years when Dr. Fooks moved into the property in the 1940s. Although the mill is derelict, the water supply in 1980 seemed to be undamaged, a feature by then unique to the Bromsgrove mills. This may be because the pool was twice dredged during the twentieth century; once by German prisoners of war.

8. Townsend Mill (Vales Mill)

Although the best known and most complete mill remaining in Bromsgrove, in 1980 Townsend was derelict and dangerous. It was in the Bridgman family from 1873 to 1955 grinding flour under Jabez Bridgman senior until his death in 1900. His wife carried on the business grinding animal feed, helped by her fifteen year old son, another Jabez, who gradually took over. He stayed to work the mill supplying sharps and other animal fodder to local farmers until he retired in 1955. Water power was used until about 1950.

Before 1873 there was a series of millers at Townsend; John Veal (1840), W. Matthews (1850s), Joseph Smith (1856), Thomas Jones (1870), and John Weaver (1871). The mill pond was once well stocked with trout and provided good fishing.

9. Crabmill

As an inn the Crabmill dates from before 1800. No records of a watermill have been found and it seems likely that the 'crabmill' may have been a cider press, possibly horse powered.

10. Blackmore Mill (Strand Mill)

Blackmore Mill stands back from the Birmingham Road just north of Davenal House. The brick building, and chimney behind it, date from 1880 when William Llewellyn, a corn dealer at the Roundabout House in the Market Place, rebuilt it to produce his 'A1 Pastry Flour'. Although the chimney, complete with his initials, implies steam power, he continued to use some water power which was a common practice in water/steam conversions. In 1896, after passing through the hands of corn dealers Henry Wilson and T. Richardson, the days of corn grinding at Blackmore were over. The mill became a nail factory, then a cycle factory and in 1903 the Worcestershire Model Laundry Limited. This laundry continued to serve Bromsgrove and district until the 1960s.

Before William Llewellyn rebuilt it there was a smaller mill there run by James Parry (miller) and John Clapton (sawyer). Clapton's career at the mill was varied but short-lived. He partnered Parry as a sawyer in 1868, but in 1870 described himself as 'cowkeeper, sawmill proprietor and beerseller' at 'The Old Water Mill'. His wife carried on his side of the business after his death in the early 1870s but gradually Parry took over to become a 'milkseller, miller and sawyer' himself in 1875. All trace of the earlier building has gone.

11. Hedges Mill

Hedges Mill was not a proper watermill but merely a waterwheel set in the Spadesbourne in the 1900s. The stream is now paved over at the site just south of Davenal House. It belonged to William Hedges, an engineer, who used it to pump water to his house which stood adjacent, and to power some light machinery.

12. The Town Mill

The Town, or Kings, Mill was on Mill Lane in the centre of Bromsgrove. It was once part of the Manor of Bromsgrove, becoming separated in 1609 when James I gave away the Manor but retained the mill for himself – thus the name Kings Mill. Its history between 1609 and the early nineteenth century is unclear. The mill became part of the Rectory Manor and, as such, was leased to the Earl of Plymouth from 1825 until about 1880. During this period, like most mills, it had several millers including William Martin (1865), the Martins were also at Moat Mill, Francis Roberts (1866), Frederick Brooke (1869) and Joseph Milton (formerly of the Lint mill, in 1880). In 1881 Bromsgrove Local Board bought the mill for £350 in order to build Market Street. The mill was pulled down and the pool drained. John Cotton observed the demolition in progress and sketched it. His picture faces page 53. It is ironic that what was probably the oldest mill in Bromsgrove was the first to disappear.

13. Moat Mill

Moat Mill standing on the Spadesbourne near the junction of Charford and Worcester Road was so called because of the ancient moat which formed part of the mill pool. It was a mill of some importance, powered by two waterwheels and housing five pairs of grindstones. The building stood until the 1950s when the site was used for a housing estate.

A flour mill, Moat Mill was run by Thomas Harrison from 1820 to 1835 (he was later at Whitford Mill), the Martin family from 1840 to 1865 and William Smith from 1870 to 1880. It is curious that in the 1880s the mill was second choice for millers whose previous mills had been destroyed – Frederick Brooke from the Town Mill and Mr. Finney of Aston Fields Steam Mills came there after his premises were burnt down in 1888.

The last miller at Moat Mill was J. W. Godsall, the baker, in 1913. Parts of the buildings were used for various purposes including a cider store for Mr. C. H. Lambe who had a haulage business there at the beginning of the twentieth century and as a woodwork shop as is described in the chapter about Bromsgrove Guild. During the First World War it provided extra capacity for the Lint Mill next door.

14. The Lint Mill

The Lint Mill in Charford continued production well into the twentieth century on the site which is Bromsgrove South High School. In the 1830s and 1840s it was variously described as a corn and worsted mill, as a corn and carding mill and a corn and woollen mill. From 1854 to 1872 when Joseph Milton was miller it was a corn mill only. In 1875 William Taylor rebuilt the mill as a Boracic Lint Mill which became a well known landmark and source of employment in Bromsgrove. It had a number of changes of ownership, from 1896 William Corbett, then another William Taylor until 1908, when the larger firm of Southall Brothers and Barclay took over. It prospered with numerous extensions and improvements until the Second World War.

The Domesday Book records that Bromsgrove, even then, had three watermills. The Town Mill was almost certainly one of them and the reader must decide for himself which may have been the other two. In 1980, of all the mills upon which over many centuries the prosperity of Bromsgrove has depended, only Townsend Mill remains with its machinery. An exhaustive list of that machinery was made by H. E. S. Simmons when he surveyed it in 1944 and it was still there in 1980, though the building which houses it is derelict and dangerous. It is to be hoped that efforts made to preserve this last representation of Bromsgrove's water power are successful to keep history alive for generations to come.

(It has since been converted for residential use. Ed.)

Author's note. I would like to acknowledge help, advice and material from Dr. D. G. Tucker and the Midlands Wind and Water Mills group; also help from Mr. R. B. Brotherton.

Jonathan Briggs

Chapter Six

Nailmaking

by Bill Kings

'Men at Work' – but nailing was for women and children too!
From an illustration in Pearsons Magazine in 1896.

6

Toil, toil and work by the furnace heat,
While our voices chime with the hammer's beat,
And our brows are crown'd with the burning sweat;
The anvil rings with each crushing blow,
And the iron is bright from the fiery glow;
One, two; one, two; that, boys, will do,
Now bend it, now heat it, now shout 'all hail!
For a thorough good work – a Bromsgrove Nail.'

Toil, toil, and work by the bellows' song:
Our faces are black, and our backs are strong,
And our arms are nervous as twisted thong,
See how the iron glows amidst the bellows' sound;
Quick and sharp fall the blows as the sparks fly around,
One, two; one, two; hark! how the hammers sing,
And round the busy workshop ring;
One, two; one, two; that, boys, will do,
Now shape it, now head it, now shout, 'all hail!
For a thorough good work – a Bromsgrove Nail'.

(Traditional. Collected by William Cotton)

The exact origins of nailmaking in Bromsgrove are obscure. It is not known why or when the trade came to the town. The earliest reference so far found is in the fourteenth century records of the Stratford-upon-Avon Guild, and the first mention of nailing in Bromsgrove is in the Parish Register for 1672. But for over a hundred years during the eighteenth and nineteenth centuries the hand-wrought nail trade was Bromsgrove's staple industry, largely supplanting the old linen and woollen cloth industries. At the beginning of the nineteenth century the nailers were a fairly prosperous group and earned as much as 15 shillings (75p) per week. But after the invention of the 'Ewbank Patent Nailing Machine' in 1832 nailers became progressively poorer through the competition of the much more productive machines. Towards the end of the century they were still earning only as much money as the nailers had a hundred years earlier. The machine could cut as many as 57,000 nails an hour. By contrast the record for making nails by hand, set by Bill Jefferies of Sidemoor, was 40,000 in a fortnight – and he worked six days a week and twelve to fourteen hours a day to do it!

It is therefore no surprise that Bromsgrove's nailers became poorer. At first there was no alternative trade and those men who could not get work as a nailer had to 'go for a soldier'. But there were some changes to come. Mr. John Collett, a linen cloth manufacturer, went out of business in 1810 and his mill was taken over by Benjamin Sanders who had patented a machine for making buttons. By 1840 he was employing some four hundred 'girls' and a few men. The button factory has been a part of Bromsgrove's industrial scene ever since. In the 1840s too the railway workshops started to provide work for men and fifty years later came the Guild. Neither could take up the same numbers as the nailing trade which in 1778 had employed nearly a thousand people. As in the early nineteenth century its ancient linen industry declined, Bromsgrove became almost a one trade town – nailing. It was not really until Herbert Austin started up his motor works at Longbridge that Bromsgrove's workforce could be reasonably sure of finding a job outside the nailing trade. That was in 1906, but, even then, nailmaking persisted as a major occupation in the town until the 1930s when there were still two hundred nailers – mostly middle aged or older – in Bromsgrove. Even after the Second World War there were still a few and the last, Charles Troth, did not die until 1959.

Nailmaking was a family trade; not just the man but his wife and children had to work in the nailshop. The whole family, which might number as many as sixteen, usually lived in a 'one up – one down' cottage rented from a nailmaster. Some houses – like Thrift Cottage in Sidemoor – were freehold, but the cost of such a property, £50 in the nineteenth century, would be beyond the normal resources of a nailer. The rent of the cottage would be about two shillings and sixpence (12^1/2p) a week. At the side of the cottage was a nailshop with three 'blocks' and here the family would spend the whole of the working day. Families were close-knit, many living in the lower part of High Street, Worcester Street, Hanover Street and St. John's Street, and many keeping a pig and some hens as well! As sewage and rubbish went straight into the Spadesbourne their lives were insanitary and unhealthy. It is not surprising that the more prosperous Bromsgrovians preferred to live at the top end of the town where the brook was less polluted.

Of the many families that can be traced in the 1851 Census Enumerators' returns is that of Joseph Rose, mentioned in an earlier chapter. Aged 56 he lived in St. John's Street with his 44 year old wife and their family. The eldest son, a cordwainer, was 29. He was the Sexton but nailers were his neighbours on all sides. With so many children in a small house it was a free-for-all in the morning, all the children dressing from a common pile, and the waking cry was 'First down's best dressed!'

The organisation of the nailing industry was markedly different from what one would expect today. The nailers bought iron from the nailmasters, together with small pieces of coke known as 'breeze' used as fuel in the nailing hearths, made the iron up into nails in the workshops adjoining their cottages, and then returned the nails in exchange for more materials. The nailers were paid entirely on piece-work and there were customary prices for the different kinds of nail; an 'elevenpenny nail' would be one paid for at eleven pence per thousand. Even then nailers could not be sure always that they would receive full value; in some cases nailers would be paid in tokens or 'truck' which could only be exchanged in certain shops (often owned by the nailmasters) where prices were high. If the nails were poor the nailer might have to go to a 'nailfogger', a middle-man who would pay less than the normal rate. After being paid the nailers would let themselves go in the twenty seven pubs along the main streets from the Crabmill to the Black Cross and beyond. Their wives' recreation came in the form of bearing enormous families, then quite usual.

The process of nailmaking never changed in the centuries during which Bromsgrove was the centre of the trade. For the simple nails there were four stages which could be completed in a matter of seconds. Depending on the type, the more complex nails would probably need one more operation. In the first stage the iron rod from which the nails were forged would be heated in the fire, kept going by bellows, on a brick hearth slightly below waist level. The second stage was to draw out the 'tang', or point, using the 'oliver' – a treadle hammer. From twelve to twenty blows might be needed. Next the nail would be half cut off the rod with a chisel, or 'hardy' and finally it was completely cut off the rod and, quickly, before it got cool, it was 'yodded'. This meant putting the head on the nail by hammering with the 'oliver'. A continuous cycle of work was maintained by having three irons in the fire at once. Hence, no doubt, the expression 'I've got more than one iron in the fire'. The heavier and more complex nails, including horse- and mule-shoe nails, spike nails, rose heads, clouts, flooring nails, miner's and alpine clinkers, and fancy welsh would be made by the men. The women made the small and simple nails such as sparrowbills, tacks, brush nails and hobs for boots.

The coming of the nailmaking machines naturally reduced the demand for the dearer hand-made nails. Making nails by hand gradually

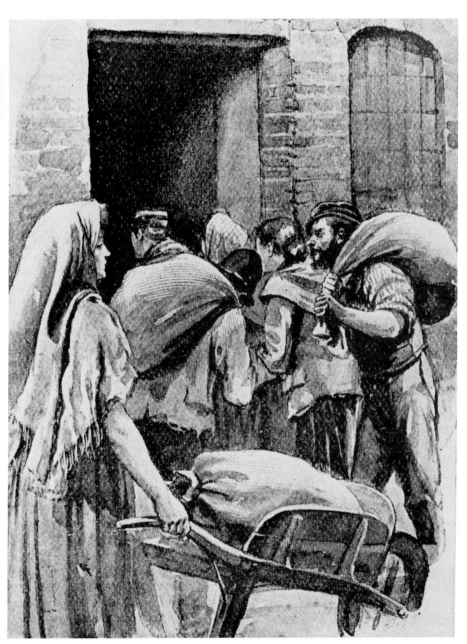

Delivering the nails to the nailmaster. From an illustration in Pearsons Magazine in 1896.

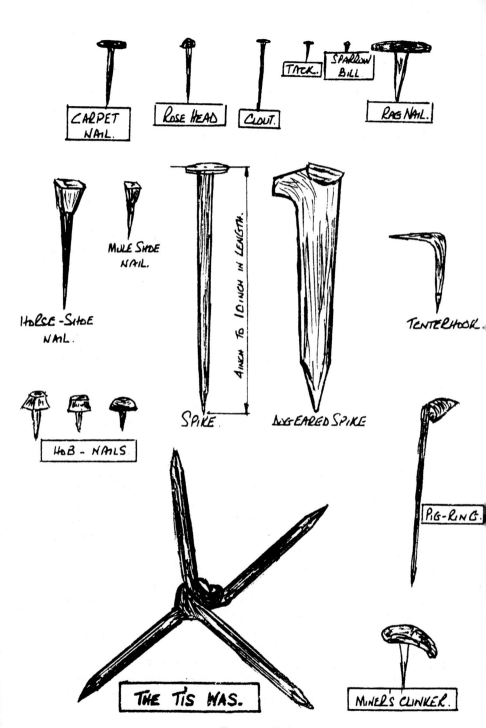

Bromsgrove Nails.

disappeared altogether in the Black Country, leaving Bromsgrove as the centre for making those nails, like the alpine clinker for mountaineering boots, which still could not be made by machine.

It has already been said that in about 1800 the nailers were reasonably well off, but ninety years later they were still only earning the same wage and those in other industries had increased substantially. Details of the change appeared in a series of articles in Pearsons Magazine in 1896 under the heading 'The White Slaves of England'. The second of these dealt specifically with the plight of the Bromsgrove nailers and gave a typical family budget for a nailer's family – a small one with only five children. Of their fifteen shillings a week more than half went on food. Bread with margarine to spread on it came alone to five shillings. Working expenses for tools and firing took another two shillings. The only hint of luxury was sixpence (2^{1}/2p) spent on tobacco. Little indeed was left for emergencies such as medical treatment.

For fifty years from 1840, a decade after the introduction of the 'Ewbank Patent Nailing Machine', the history of nailing in Bromsgrove consists of a fight to maintain the customary prices and to resist the repeated cuts imposed by the nailmasters. Between 1842 and 1891 there were seven major strikes in the industry. The first was in 1842 against a proposal to cut prices by 10%. The Black Country was then still the centre of hand-nailing as the machine was only just beginning to bite into the nailer's livelihood. Nailers in both Bromsgrove and the Black Country struck and 15,000 of them attended a meeting in Dudley Market Place – 1,500 of them had walked from Bromsgrove. Trouble was expected and in the days before the civilian police force was properly established the army was used to control public gatherings. The nailers, perhaps recalling the Peterloo massacre in Manchester in 1819 when people were cut down by a Yeomanry sabre charge, brought caltrops, which were known locally as the 'tis-was'. These have four outward facing spikes so that one always points upwards when they are thrown on the ground. These are an effective weapon against cavalry so that when the 6th Hussars were sent in to disperse the nailers they were well prepared to defend themselves. After ten weeks of strike the nailers were forced back to work without any gain.

The next thirty years saw three long strikes. In 1860 both the Bromsgrove and the Black Country nailers were out for twenty weeks and again in 1868 they were out for twelve. In 1869 the 'Starvation List' of prices (cutting them by a further 20%) led to a ten week strike. In Bromsgrove the strike began with a meeting of 4,500 in Crown Close when a Nailers Union was founded and the nailers agreed not to teach their children to make nails. But after ten weeks the strike was broken and the need for earnings sent the nailers back to their nailing blocks. The lack of employment, except from the railway, meant that the children still had to learn the trade and receive the traditional bright new penny when they made their first nail. Eight years later a further 10% cut produced a strike for twenty weeks and the next year, 1878, again saw the nailers out to restore this reduction. Bromsgrove nailers were offered this after eight weeks and accepted it; but the nailmasters in the Black Country (even though they were often the same people as the Bromsgrove nailmasters) were unyielding. The Black Country nailers resented their Bromsgrove brothers split in solidarity. Nevertheless Bromsgrove nailers paid fourpence a week into a fund to support those still on strike – and the money was collected by the nailmasters themselves who paid it out to the strikers in the Black Country!

Now the conditions of the workers in the nailing industry were coming to the attention of a wider public. The 1880 Beech Report on Sweated Industries concentrated on nailmaking and chainmaking and there were frequent articles in the press describing the poverty and dreadful life endured by the nailers and their families, who were probably by now the poorest group of people in regular employment in the country. The culmination of this was the sixteen week strike in 1891/1892 which was sponsored by the Sunday Chronicle edited by Edward Hulton. The aim of the strike was to put up the customary price for nails by 50% and, in order to avoid the problems which had caused the collapse of earlier strikes, Hulton started a fund to support the nailers and their families for the duration of the strike. The first £100 came from the newspaper and, among members of the public who gave were the chainmakers of Brierley Hill, who donated £25. Payments from the fund were four shillings and sixpence (22¹/₂p) per week for men and half that sum for women. The strikers were well organised and, in addition to money, there were soup kitchens, and even entertainments and diversions; a bullock was roasted behind the Coach and Horses, and Bostocks Circus had a special performance on a Saturday afternoon with the profits going to the strike fund. Before the performance the circus processed through the streets of Birmingham and were led by the band of the 6th Hussars – that same regiment that had attempted to disperse them, or their fathers, just fifty years earlier in Dudley Market Place!

Even when the nailmasters offered 20% the nailers held out and retained the sympathy of the public. Eventually an increase of between 30% and 40% was accepted but the effect of this was to price the nailers out of the market. By now nailing had almost died out in the Black Country except by machine and hand nailing was confined to Bromsgrove. Fortunately the Guild was soon to be established and needed workers so the nailers at last were able to achieve the objectives of the 1869 strike that it 'was a crime to teach a lad nailing'. Without recruiting the industry declined and finally died in the 1950s.

Nailing was a hard trade but with a wonder of its own. The nailers were people of character and independence. They had a close family life in the alleys and entries of the town. They knew the life was hard and were not sorry to see it die without leaving a detailed record of it. There are few records of the Nailers Union or of the strike fund of 1891. But for almost three centuries nailing was a large part of the life of Bromsgrove.

Chapter Seven

Canal Mania

by John Burman

An impression of the experimental lift at Tardebigge
drawn by R. Argyle for the Bromsgrove Society.

7

Through undulating fields and down a fertile escarpment the Worcester Birmingham canal descends in purposeful steps from Tardebigge to Stoke. Born at the height of the canal mania in the last years of the eighteenth century the canal took 24 years to complete, from Worcester Bar in Birmingham to Diglis Basin in Worcester. Dominated by the Birmingham Canal Navigation (B.C.N.) and later by the rivalry of the Oxford, Worcester and Wolverhampton Railway (O.W.W.R.), this canal's fortunes waxed and waned, tugged relentlessly by the vested interests of competing companies and the market forces of the community. It is a history of high hopes and bold initiatives, of sanguine expectations and cruel disappointments; and of increasingly desperate men in the face of inevitable decline.

In 1784 a meeting was held to promote the Bilston Worcester canal. The plan was to link the Stourbridge and Dudley canals with Diglis on the River Severn. The canal was to run through Bromsgrove. It would have been 26 miles long with two tunnels and 128 locks. The pressure for such a canal was clamant. The Birmingham Canal Navigation bestrode the hub of the waterway system like a giant spider. Coal from Dudley had to travel through the B.C.N. to Wolverhampton, and then by the Staffs and Worcester canal to Stourport in order to reach the Severn. How much better to travel direct? Despite vigorous opposition from the B.C.N., but with strong support from Lord Dudley, a Bill was promoted in Parliament. In 1786 Aris's Gazette reported rejoicing and bell ringing in Wolverhampton; the Lords had rejected the Bill.

Four years later, in January 1790, a public meeting was held in Bromsgrove. The intention now was to build a barge canal between Birmingham and Worcester. The B.C.N. objected and refused both water and access across a seven foot strip of brickwork, the famous Worcester Bar at Gas Street Basin, not to be removed for another 25 years; until then all goods had to be transhipped across the bar. By now, however, the political momentum was too great for such a scheme to be denied and the following year the Worcester Birmingham Canal Promotion Bill became law. A local poet sprang into verse in Aris's Gazette. Too awful to reproduce in full, here is one verse:

> "Redditch where sons of the needle reside
> Who commerce revere and make friendship their pride
> The prospect enraptures – and Bromsgrove no less,
> Has cause at the victory joy to express."

Work on the canal began quickly. Surveyed by John Snape and Josiah Clowes, it was engineered by Thomas Cartwright, and later by John Woodhouse of the Tardebigge Lift fame. William Crossley completed the job. By May 1797 the canal had reached Hopwood, the 2,750 yard tunnel at Wast Hill having been dug. Here it paused for lack of finance. Dr. Thomas Cooper, treasurer, was found to be owing the Company £ 13,800. He resigned. Fund raising progressed and by 1807 the canal had been dug to Tardebigge – the Old Wharf. This featured a 'commodious basin, wharf, weighing machine, etc. all prepared for the accommodation of trade'. It also featured a pub, The Navigation, of which more later.

Tardebigge was the first real moneyspinner for the canal. Trade was developed between Bromsgrove, Droitwich, Worcester, Redditch, Alcester, Alvechurch and Evesham. In 1808 Thomas Sherrat, a Birmingham carrier, advertised transport by water to Tardebigge and thence by land to Worcester; and a variety of other schemes were on offer. A packet boat plied between Alvechurch and Birmingham. Tolls and charges yielded a satisfactory £3,500 only fifteen months after the opening and the company paid its first dividend.

The next stage was the escarpment; a regular decline over 16 miles to Worcester. The engineers and the company were divided. Locks were simpler and well proven – but they were expensive in water. Fifty eight were to be built eventually. On the other hand a host of new ideas about lifts and inclined planes were abroad. John Woodhouse, the resident engineer, was an enthusiastic proponent of the new methods. A major consideration was the clause in the 1791 Act that denied water to the canal from any source but the River Severn. This clause, though honoured in its non-observance, had been inserted at the insistence of the B.C.N. and it intended that water should have to be pumped up 428 feet from the river.

A comparative estimate of finishing the canal with lifts or locks, together with the relative annual running costs, was drawn up. It reads like a modern balance sheet. In January of 1808 the Company authorised

Woodhouse to build an experimental lift at Tardebigge. He was to pay for
it out of his own pocket. It is best described by Rolt:

"The Tardebigge Lift consisted of a single wooden caisson 70 foot long,
8 foot wide, and 4½ foot deep, weighing 64 tons when filled with water.
This caisson was supported by rods attached to chains which passed over
cast iron pulley wheels, each of 12 foot diameter. There were four of these
pulley wheels on each side, each set revolving on a common horizontal axle
mounted on an overhead framework. Counterbalance weights, consisting
of masses of brickwork stacked in timber frames and weighing 8 tons each,
hung by chains on the landward side of the pulleys. Chains of equal weight
were hung beneath the casement and the counterweight frames. This was
an ingenious arrangement, for hanging suspended or lying slack on the
ground as the lift was moved, they exactly counterpoised the weight of the
suspended chain which would otherwise have thrown the lift out of balance
as their length varied. The lift was operated manually by a windlass which
rotated the pulleys through gearing. Gates enclosed the caisson and the
canal at either end and a sluice valve admitted water to the space between
each set in order to relieve the pressure and enable them to be opened."

In February 1809 a public trial commenced. The excitement must have
been considerable, the lift having incurred both enthusiasm and
opprobrium. Fifty boats were passed on the first day in 6 hours and 29
minutes; and on the nineteenth and last day 113 boats in 12 hours. The
great canal engineers were consulted. William Jessop was in favour and
tried to form a company to adopt the lifting machine. But the final arbiter
was Sir John Rennie and his report rings true across the decades.

"The lift does not in fact perform better than I expected it would for
the short time and in the manner it has been done, and, I doubt not, if
carefully attended, it will work for a considerable time to come. My
objections are that it is too complex, too delicate in its parts and requires
more attention and careful management than can possibly be expected to
be given when in general use on a canal; that its parts are subject to
frequent derangement and the repairs consequent thereon will be very
heavy, and the trade of the canal frequently stopped."

With hindsight he was right. The last working inclined plane ceased to
function in 1912. Had the Worcester Birmingham flight consisted of the
proposed 17 lifts the canal would probably have been derelict since the
beginning of the twentieth century.

William Crossley completed the canal in 1815. It had cost £610,000.
Earlier that year the B.C.N. relented and the Worcester Bar was replaced by

a bar lock. Through navigation was now complete. Side arms and connections to other canals were to follow but, for now, the Company flourished.

The main function of a canal is trade; and it is still, for although commercial carrying has greatly diminished, the trade in pleasure cruising has expanded to the point where there are probably more craft on the canals than at the height of the canal mania.

For Bromsgrove the canal was tantalisingly close. The focus of trade was at Tardebigge. Coal was the staple commodity. Mined in the Black Country it fuelled the furnaces, the lime kilns, the dwellings and the pumps of England. Boats streamed out of the Black Country in all directions laden with 'slack' as the 'boaties' called it. They back loaded with whatever cargo they could get, but always returned with coal. Tardebigge boasted two exceptions to this rule. Below the top lock a side arm reached 500 yards into a quarry, probably a marl pit. The other local material was limestone. It was quarried at Himbleton, brought by tramway to Dunhampstead and then by canal to lime kilns at Tardebigge – fuelled of course by coal from the Black Country. The lime was then sold to local farmers – often themselves boat owners. From wharfs on their land farm produce was transported into Birmingham and Worcester. T. and M. Dixon, yeoman farmers on Lord Plymouth's estate and entrepreneurs extraordinary, were doing this until the 1930s; latterly on their boat the 'Enterprise'. Less savoury cargoes included manure into Birmingham and night soil out. This was tipped at Lane House Wharf, just beyond Bittel and was spread over adjacent fields. The roses luxuriate in the gardens at the bottom of Aqueduct Lane!

Several brickyards developed on the canal. Both slack and local clay came by boat and the bricks were back loaded. The last load to Wynn's brickyard at Alvechurch was in 1926.

The demands of the trade led to further attempts to improve the navigation. The Upper and Lower Bittel reservoirs were constructed; the Upper as a canal feeder, the Lower at the insistence of, and for the convenience of, the mill owners on the River Arrow. The Company, however, intended to retrieve its water and installed a modified Watt's beam engine. A side arm was dug to supply the machine with fuel. This was known as Jacob's Cut, the last load of slack being delivered in 1911. The pump itself was dismantled in the First World War and sent to Wales. Only the ivy clad engine house remains. In the 1850s schemes were proposed to construct side arms to connect the canal from Tardebigge to Bromsgrove and Redditch, but both were opposed by landowners and failed.

It is difficult to engender interest in the study of decline. The growth and development of a project is so much more motivating. Yet the story of the decline of the Worcester Birmingham canal has a fascination of its own because it records the manoeuvres of beleagured men, trapped in an economic pattern, powerless as it turned out, but always striving to find a way. Their first procedures were to renegotiate tolls, cut prices and improve the navigation. Next they tried diversification. The third ploy was to merge; first with the Droitwich and later with the Coombe Hill canals, the former to promote the salt trade, and the latter to conserve the coal trade to Cheltenham. Both foundered. The final blow that crippled the navigation came from the Dunhampstead line of the Oxford, Worcester and Wolverhampton Railway. The railway story is told elsewhere in this book. Other desperate schemes were attempted, but in 1868 the Company had to appoint a receiver.

In 1874 the canal was bought by the Gloucester and Berkeley Canal Company and renamed the Sharpness New Docks and Gloucester and Birmingham New Canal. The new company set to work with vigour, improving the works and dredging, but the pattern of decline continued unchecked, and it was only four more years before it too failed to make ends meet. For nearly seventy years the canal slumbered; but after the Second World War it awoke with the British Waterways Board maintaining the navigation for an increasing variety of pleasure craft. Many people have discovered on the waterways a quiet and lovely countryside unknown to those who only travel on tarmac.

There are usually pubs aplenty along a canal. The Tardebigge flight, however, is famous for its abstinence. Two pubs have closed. The Navigation which was at Tardebigge Old Wharf boasts the questionable distinction of having been closed because of drunkenness. None of the main tunnels have tow paths and boatmen legged, railed, or shafted their way through, while the horse was taken over the top. Legging is a method whereby two men lie on a plank stretched across the fore-peak and propel the boat by walking along the sides of the tunnel. It is a cold and dangerous job and the men who plied this trade were paid a small fee by the boatmen. The leggers rested in a small shed by the mouth of the tunnel – or better still in The Navigation. Drunkenness was often the rule. Tardebigge tunnel is cut through sandstone and only partly brick lined. The wet fissured walls provided an uncertain grip for the leggers' hob nailed boots; and few of them could swim. When a second legger drowned, unsteadied by drink, the Lord of the Manor, 'well acquainted with the complaints of fighting and drunkenness' closed the pub and demolished it.

The other pub to close was the Halfway House. Strategically placed by lock 41 it marks the halfway stage of the flight of locks from Tardebigge to Stoke. This was a real boaties' pub whose hours were regulated solely by demand. The proprietor, Tom Thompson, drew his last pint in 1959. His barrels of Aux's Ales stood coolly in the cellar and he drew from them in jugs. He hated to waste a journey down the cellar steps and would pause halfway down to enquire if his customer would be drinking "one pint or two?"

The fastest passage of the 36 locks from Tardebigge to Stoke is credited to Steerer Merrel and his two sons. Deprived of drink all morning they meant to be at the Navigation at Stoke before the towels went over. They left Tardebigge in an unladen salt boat at mid-day and in the jargon of the cut, 'He had a good road. He whipped up the donkeys in the pounds and strapped the top gates'. They were supping ale by a quarter to two.

Horses, mules or donkeys powered the boats. The boatmen called them 'animals' indiscriminately. Donkeys were preferred on the Worcester Birmingham, not only because they drew a boat quicker, but because they could be loaded in the fore section of the boat, with the coal piled high against the lee-boards astern, for the river tow to Gloucester. They were harnessed in tandem and were inveterately lazy. George Bate, B.E.M. of Tardebigge, who retired in 1968 after 53 years work on the canal, was the fourth generation of his family to work on canal maintenance. His great grandfather had started with the canal company as a blacksmith when it opened. George told of how he dusted his animals beneath their tails with a bunch of nettles to urge them on. "They fair trotted to Gas Street", he said, "That evening while I was stabling them, they kicked me – in unison. I was sore for a week!"

The Queens Head at Stoke Pound is a pub which pre-dates the canal era. It was originally the Blacksmiths Arms and the forge stood until the 1960s. Like the canal its use has changed with the times and was, indeed, extended in the 1970s to cater for the pleasure boat trade.

When James Brindley completed the Staffs and Worcester canal it joined the Severn at a tiny hamlet called Lower Mitton. Today it is Stourport. What changes might there have been had the Worcester Birmingham canal, as originally proposed, run through Bromsgrove?

Chapter Eight

Bromsgrove and the Lickey Incline
The Railway Revolution

by the Rev. W. Awdry

THE LICKEY INCLINED PLANE
BIRMINGHAM AND GLOUCESTER RAILWAY
CAPTN W. S. MOORSOM, ENGR.
The Philadelphia Engine ascending the Plane rising one in 37 with a Train of Loaded Wagons the total
weight moved 74 Tons – The maximum Speed $9^{3}/_{4}$ Miles Per Hour June 1849

Dolby's well known engraving is reproduced with the permission of the Science Museum.

8

Earlier chapters of this book have emphasised the importance of Bromsgrove as a transport centre from those times when its High Street was part of the salt track and it was a cross roads for the drovers, to the nineteenth century, by which time it had become a key town for stage coaches on many of their routes. The previous chapter has told of the impact canal transport had on the commerce of the district. The coming of the railway virtually ruined both these older forms of transport and specially interesting developments in railway engineering were born here. This chapter will tell the story of those early pioneering days. But first it may be as well to give the true facts which led to the erection of those two famous gravestones in Bromsgrove's churchyard.

The gravestones give a most misleading impression. People assume that a Norris engine exploded and that Scaife and Rutherford were her driver and fireman. Both assumptions are wrong. The engine which exploded was a tank engine named, perhaps aptly, 'Surprise'. She had been built in Birmingham by John Inshaw to the design of a certain Dr. Church, and a Mr. Goddard also of Birmingham, had footed the bill. They had tried unsuccessfully to sell her to the London & Birmingham and the Grand Junction Railways, so they offered her at a knock down price to the Birmingham & Gloucester (B & G) who agreed to try her out in November 1840. She was unconventional even for those days, and as she stood over the ashpit at Bromsgrove after a day's run, Thomas Scaife, a bank engine driver and Joseph Rutherford, Works Foreman, were curious enough to stroll across to chat with John Inshaw and his son Paul who were crewing her. The Inshaws left the footplate to let Scaife and Rutherford climb on. The explosion came without warning and Scaife and Rutherford were picked up some twenty five yards away. Scaife was killed outright, but Rutherford died the next morning. Since Scaife was a bank-engine driver it is probable that his engine, the 'Boston' (No. 14), is shown on his stone, while Rutherford had one of the smaller (8 ton) Norrises on his. Incidentally the restoration of the stones, though carefully and lovingly done, is incorrect in one detail. The small (Class B) Norrises never carried

A huge success!

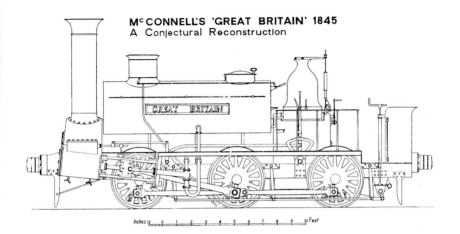

The Great Britain. Made in Bromsgrove.

An absolute disaster!

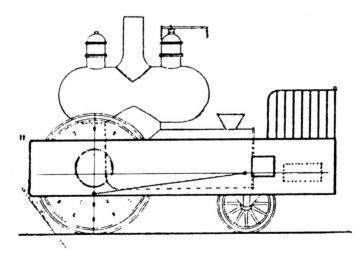

The Surprise. Made in Birmingham.

Conjectural drawings of engines by Col. Whitcombe and the late P. C. Dewhurst reproduced by permission of the Historical Model Railway Society and the Public Record Office respectively.

A result of the disaster.

The gravestones in Bromsgrove Churchyard.

Photo of gravestones by Rev. W. Awdry.

the sandbox dome which was fitted to the 12 ton bank engines. T. R. Perkins, an acute observer who visited Bromsgrove in 1904, remarks, "A curious fact... is that one of the engines possesses a dome on the boiler barrel while the other is without that appendage".

Norris engines – like soap flakes and detergents! – came in three sizes: Small (Class B weighing 8 tons), Medium (Class A of 10 tons), and the Large 'economy' size which was 12 tons. In all the Birmingham & Gloucester had 17 Norrises (9 B's, 3 A's and 5 of the 12 ton A Extras). They also had nine other Class A's which were built for them in England. But why were American engines chosen?

The promoters of the B & G, in their inexperience, made many expensive 'economies', but their most expensive one was to insist on a straight line up the Lickey for two and a half miles at a gradient of 1 in 37½ in order to save on the cost of the increased mileage necessary to avoid it. Their 'economy' here kept the company virtually in the red throughout its independent existence and has bedevilled operation ever since. Captain Moorsom, their engineer who laid out the incline under protest, was nevertheless nettled by caustic remarks about it from Brunel and Stephenson and was determined to work it by adhesion just to prove them wrong. He had seen a trade catalogue from Norris of Philadelphia. This recorded the spectacular hill climbing feats of Norris engines. So he opened negotiations for "the trial, and if successful, the purchase of one engine on condition of taking 10 more engines of sizes useful to the company".

An 8 ton (Class B) engine, 'England', duly came over and failed her test. This was not surprising for the Directors insisted that she be worked at 55 lbs per sq. inch measured by an independent gauge, whereas Norrises in America usually worked at a nominal 60 lbs pressure but which was actually nearer 90 lbs. The Directors promptly declared the deal off. This brought William Gwynn, Norris' agent, hot-foot to Birmingham to explain that the despatch of the smaller engine had been a mistake and that the larger engine, now on the way, would be sure to meet their requirements. If she did the B & G would, he was sure, be kind enough to buy her and the smaller Norrises as well.

The Class A (10 ton) 'Victoria' arrived, and failed her tests for the same reason. The Directors again called the deal off. This was in November 1839, and with the line scheduled to open in June 1840 the locomotive situation was getting pretty desperate. They told Gwynn in round terms what they thought of him and Norris; so, after giving them a week or so to cool off, Gwynn returned, and this time bound Norris to supply a 12 ton engine which incidentally had never left Norris' drawing board! If this loco was successful the Directors would, he felt sure, be honour bound to buy not only the 'Victoria' but also all the Class B Norrises which had been sent over and stored in Liverpool.

The 12 tonner named 'Philadelphia' arrived in May 1840 and proved successful on the Lickey. She was given the number 13 and is shown in Dolby's well known picture on the title page. John Donahue, one of Norris' men, came over with her and stayed many years with the B & G. Philadelphia was always his engine. Another A Extra, the 'Boston' arrived in August so Captain Moorsom felt it was safe to open up from Bromsgrove to Cofton Hackett in September. The third A Extra, 'William Gwynn' arrived in December 1840 in charge of another American Fitter/ Driver named Israel York. He too stayed with the Company. He and Donahue lodged at the Vigo, an ale-house near bridge 106 south of Blackwell.

The Lickey was, from the first, recognised as a potential danger spot and worked with military discipline. Captain Moorsom drew up a code of rules and trained a corps of brakesmen to take complete charge of trains descending. The code is too long to quote, but here are some of the salient points. All drivers of southbound trains had to close regulator at Bridge 109 at Linthurst. It was then a timber structure and was painted white so as to be unmistakeable. Having shut off steam the driver whistled his approach and stopped dead at a white post set up beside the down line some 300 yards from the top of the plane. This post, or its successor, was still there in 1980, but had been moved at some date unknown to the lineside fence. The brakesmen then took charge. The First, or Chief, Brakesman was Captain of the train for its 'voyage' down the bank. He sat on the middle coach and directed operations. The Second Brakesman examined the brakes on every coach and saw that they were manned by guards or travelling porters. He then took his seat on the leading coach. When all was ready the Captain, with one blast of his whistle, ordered the driver to open up just enough to start the train, while the fireman stood to his tender brake. Once on the move two whistle blasts meant 'shut off steam and let her roll' while three called for a general brake application; five blasts announced 'Obstruction – Danger!' Passenger trains were limited to 20 miles per hour and goods trains to 10 mph. The brakesmen had nothing to do with ascending trains.

When the policeman's bell announced the approach of an Up train to Bromsgrove, the big Norris would proceed along the centre road in the station, cross to the Up line and stand under the bridge. The train would draw in behind and the banker's fireman would couple up. Meanwhile the station policeman inspected all vehicles brakes and couplings. Only when satisfied could he let the guard give the 'Right away'. In May 1841 the Gloucester Mechanics Institute hired a train for an excursion to Birmingham. They arrived at Bromsgrove with 623 passengers in 23 coaches hauled by two engines. The train was divided, and the first portion was sent up with one of the train engines and a banker. "But" wrote the Chronicle reporter, "the pantings of the two engines so nearly resembled the puffings of broken winded horses, that... the engine which was to have assisted the second portion was sent... to chase the train, buffer up, and push...". This was exceptional; the B & G rarely banked in rear, nearly always in front. But hair raising manoeuvres happened at Summit; hazardous enough to give any modern railwayman heart attacks!

Let the rules speak for themselves: Rules 7 and 8 (Ascending). 'As soon as the tail of the train reaches the summit... the fireman of the bank engine will throw off (sic) his engine from the train, and at the same moment the train engine is to slacken speed by shutting off steam, thus allowing the bank engine to go at least 30 yards ahead, and turn into the siding prepared for the purpose'.

Consider the frightful hazards; four separate people are involved in a complicated operation needing split second timing. This timing depended on a number of variables – length and speed of train, condition of the rails, time of day and light conditions, to say nothing of the vagaries of the weather. The fireman had to clamber over the rear of his tender, then, standing on a buffer shank, he had to hold on with one hand while lifting the coupling with the other. The pointsman, however, is not mentioned, yet he was the kingpin of the whole, and had to act with split second timing to get the banker into the spur, and the train following it safely away to Birmingham.

From time to time the rules were changed as a result of experience. On 19 May 1841, for instance, a goods train failed to stop at Bromsgrove platform and rammed the waiting banker. Rule 3 (Ascending) was then altered to prohibit bankers from waiting under the bridge. They had to stand on the centre road till the train had stopped; but firemen still continued to risk their lives several times a day at Summit until, in 1842, J. E. McConnell invented and fitted a slip coupling to all bank engines. Firemen could uncouple their engines by using a lever on the footplate.

Another Lickey anecdote comes to mind. In the third week of August 1841 Edward Bury invited himself to Bromsgrove and challenged the B & G

Locomotive Department to a test. Bury was at that time a prominent man in locomotive affairs, and knew it! He was Locomotive Superintendent of the London and Birmingham and had his own engine factory at Liverpool. He descended on Bromsgrove with one of his latest models, a 0-4-0 goods engine, and a test train of seven vehicles and a coach filled with people he had invited to witness his triumph. At Bromsgrove he announced to all and sundry that anything a yankee engine could do one of his could do better. But alas for Bury's confidence, his engine refused with seven of his wagons and again with six; she stalled after 270 yards with four (31½ tons); only when a further wagon had been removed reducing the load to some 24 tons could it reach the summit at 8.7 miles per hour. Philadelphia, the big Norris, coped comfortably with any load offered, blowing off all the way. It was only with the lighter loadings that she fell behind and this was only in speed. Bury was furious, and his chagrin was increased when he realised too late that only with Philadelphia's help could he get his train back to Birmingham that evening! Philadelphia's victory was decisive, and for the next four years the supremacy of the big Norrises on the Lickey was unchallenged. But they were expensive brutes, their appetite for coke was enormous, and as two out of the three had to be kept in steam for sixteen hours a day each revenue earning trip up the two and half miles of the Lickey incline cost seventeen shillings and fivepence (87½p). It was not until the second half of 1842, when rebuilding had increased their haulage capacity and more than halved their running costs that they began to be an asset to the Company instead of an expensive necessity. But this is to anticipate the story of their rebuilding. It is time to turn to the Locomotive Works.

Captain Moorsom considered rightly that the foot of the incline was where reserve locomotive power would be needed. He planned accordingly, and in June 1839 land was bought at Aston Fields for station buildings, cottages and Locomotive Works. His plans were passed in July and contracts let; building began in August. There was to be stabling within the building for some twelve engines on the east side, with repair bays for as many more on the west, together with a stationary engine, Turnery, Brass foundry, Smith's shops etc on the ground floor; a second storey was to house a Drawing office and a Pattern maker's and Joiner's shops. Work went well ahead till the Committee got financial jitters in October and stopped all work in December. Work was resumed in April 1840 and a burst of furious energy and overtime was needed to get something ready by the time the Bromsgrove Cheltenham section opened in June. The building was reduced to one storey only and at ground level one half, the northern part, of the original plan was built. The shell was ready by June but there had been no tooling up. Such repair equipment as there was was of a 'Make do and mend' variety devised by Rutherford and his Superintendent William Creuze. The stationary engine, some lathes and other equipment began to trickle in by September, but locomotives, even new ones, needed constant maintenance – a slow job with primitive tools and untrained staff, and by that time the yard was choked with cripples deteriorating outside as there was no room for them in the truncated building.

Creuze gave up the struggle and took refuge in drink. Only Rutherford battled on inducing reluctant locomotives to run the trains. His death in November was not only a tragedy for his family it was a disaster for the Company. Things went from bad to worse when Walworth, a drinking pal of Creuze, took Rutherford's place as foreman. Makeshift and botched repairs were the order of the day. Of this the Locomotive Committee were blissfully unaware till, in March 1841, a botched repair gave way when Creuze, Walworth and the rest of a drinking party were coming home in the small hours of the morning from a drinking session at the Vigo on the 'Boston'. Steam sprayed all over the footplate. Creuze was dead drunk and unable to move. He was scalded to death and the resulting inquest blew the lid off affairs at the works.

G. D. Bischopp, a draughtsman who had stayed clear of the Creuze/Walworth racket, was recalled from his honeymoon to take charge and James Edward McConnell, a young man of 26, was appointed Locomotive Foreman in July. He had been trained at an engineering firm in Glasgow, had worked for three years at Bury's engine factory at Liverpool, but having quarrelled with Bury in 1840, had got himself a job in Manchester. McConnell was a forceful and determined young man and it was fortunate that he and Bischopp got on well together. As a result things at the works took a decisive turn for the better. For instance, very soon a shed was being built against the east wall of the Works covering two lines of track. Inspection pits were dug, and the shed was tooled up for occasional repairs. This shed had been asked for ever since June 1840, and as often refused as an 'unnecessary expense'. Yet McConnell got it sanctioned and started within three weeks of his arrival!

McConnell, his mother, and his sister Elizabeth settled into a company house at the station. It was almost certainly the one at the north end of the terrace block, since demolished, which had been occupied first by Rutherford, and then by Walworth. A contemporary plan shows two other houses, detached and standing north and south of the cottages. Bischopp and his young wife occupied one and Henry Van Beurle, Chief Station Clerk, had the other.

At the works Bischopp and McConnell had found a daunting task. The B & G had a stud of 30 locomotives; three were virtual write-offs from the construction period, three were bank engines, and of the remainder only four could be relied upon to run the fifty one miles between Birmingham and Gloucester without breaking down en route. These were the four sturdy 2-2-2's bought in 1839 from Forrester of Liverpool. They were rostered for the mail trains, and were the only engines allowed by McConnell to run through Bromsgrove. All the rest, on trains in either direction, had to come off for examination at Bromsgrove and be replaced by others. This policy ensured that every engine was inspected at least once in three days and impending trouble was caught before it happened. This policy paid off and by January 1842 arrears of maintenance had been beaten. They could now tackle another urgent problem – the cost of working the Lickey incline.

As explained earlier bankers were costing seventeen shillings and fivepence a trip of five miles, of which only half was in revenue earning service. Not only was it necessary to keep them in steam sixteen hours a day, but when they were working flat out they made steam faster than it could be used, and wasted it by blowing off on the ascent. McConnell and Bischopp experimented with Philadelphia, rebuilding her as a saddletank engine – the first ever constructed. Water carried in the tank above the boiler, and fuel in bunkers on the footplate made her tender unnecessary and cut out its 7 tons dead weight, whilst the weight of the water and fuel on the engine herself increased the grip of her driving wheels on the rails and gave her extra haulage capacity. They found that the load limit up the incline had been increased to 80/90 tons gross. This was power and to spare for any traffic offered at the time. They also led a pipe from the safety valve to the water tank, and fitted a cock so that the driver could, when he wished, turn the waste steam into the tank thus heating the feed water and saving fuel. They also fitted, and this was an innovation at the time, screw operated brakes to her driving wheels capable of holding her anywhere on the incline. Donahue was delighted with her.

Experiments being successful, they 'saddletanked' the other two bankers and when the necessary preparations had been made at Blackwell, and the timetable changed to suit, they worked the Lickey with bankers alone from 1st May 1842. For Up trains the train engine from Gloucester would come off at Bromsgrove and the banker would come on. Once at

Summit the fireman slipped the train using his uncoupler and the banker ran to her spur. Meanwhile the Train Guards would brake the coaches to a standstill, an engine emerged from the newly built shed at Blackwell, coupled up and started for Birmingham. The banker would wait till a Down train arrived and had shed its engine. She would then leave her spur, couple to the train and take it down the incline. Thus the bankers were employed in revenue earning service in both directions and the cost per trip was more than halved. Whereas in the last half of 1841 the bankers had travelled 6,210 miles with a coke bill of £324, the coke bill for the same period in 1842 was £166 for 6,600 and the cost per bank engine trip had fallen to seven shillings and three halfpence.

Though from May 1842 bankers alone worked all service trains up and down the Lickey, there was a certain amount of gravity working too. This increased when Blackwell became a locomotive station. Engines were fuelled and watered there and coke was brought up from Bromsgrove in wagons coupled to any convenient train. The empties went down by gravity. Permanent Way Contractors sent their empty ballast wagons down by gravity too. Heavy goods trains were divided at Blackwell, the first portion being sent down with an engine, while the second part, after a suitable interval, followed by gravity – sometimes with spectacular results at Bromsgrove. For instance on 18 June 1842 the second part of a goods train collided with the first just south of the station and spread itself over both roads. The Chief Brakesman, Wells, was given a rocket and fined, but when a similar runaway happened in August he was sacked and W. H. Goodwin from the Cromford and High Peak Railway was given the job. Following these two accidents the dividing of goods trains at Blackwell was forbidden. They were to be held at Blackwell until enough brakesmen or travelling porters were available to man the brakes on every third wagon.

Gravity working for empty coke and ballast wagons continued till it too was prohibited after an accident at dusk on 23 December 1842. Mrs. Woodward, a washerwoman who was employed at a house near to the incline, had asked for, and obtained, permission to use the line as a short cut on her way home between train times. Without telling anyone, some overlookers of the Permanent Way gang used that slack time to get into a ballast wagon and career downhill on their way home. Their wagon had no lights. Mrs. Woodward did not see them, nor did they see her. They only felt the impact and were quite unable to stop. The result was an order abolishing all gravity working on and from 3 January 1843, which goes on to say, '... three wagons or less are to be attached to a returning bank-engine and any greater number must be taken down in the same way but in charge of a brakesman.' This rather suggests that Mr. Wetherall, the then General Manager, had not found it possible to devise a timetable which balanced all the Lickey workings, so that occasionally bankers had to descend 'light engine'.

In May 1842 Bischopp left the Works to take up an appointment with the Disc Engine Co. of Birmingham and McConnell reigned at the Works in his stead. He held the post until January 1847 when he was appointed to Wolverton. Much could be said of the improvements he introduced during this period and of the high standard of workmanship he demanded and got. All this was achieved with some difficulty, for in 1843 a group of dividend hungry shareholders who were largely ignorant of railway management gained partial control of the Board. Wages were slashed and any expenditure considered unnecessary was cut to the bone. But McConnell had their measure. He became skilful in presenting his needs for spare parts and other equipment as being '... in the interests of economy.' He even managed to persuade the Directors that it was 'in the interests of economy' to buy two new goods engines from Jones and Potts early in 1844. He was right too! Those two 0-6-0's built to McConnell's design were the best buys the B & G ever made in their short life. 'Bristol' and 'Hercules' coped valiantly with whatever traffic they were offered, survived the Midland take-over (1845/46), were rebuilt by Kirtley as well-tanks in 1860 and soldiered on as Lickey bankers till the turn of the century.

In his report on locomotive power at the half yearly meeting in January 1844 McConnell pointed out that the A Extras were becoming outclassed. It was true; they now had five but the loads offered were increasing and some trains were having to be divided or double-headed with consequent expense and delay. He therefore asked permission to design and build at Bromsgrove a locomotive to cope with the problem. The permission was given on 18 March 1844. There is no record of her in building. She was probably kept 'hush hush'; but when she rolled out of the works in June 1845 and did her trials she caused a sensation and was hailed as the largest locomotive in the country. She was a 0-6-0 outside cylindered saddletank and proved herself capable of tackling a load of 1,000 tons on the level and lifting 135/140 tons up 1 in 37 at a speed of eight to ten miles per hour. Her dimensions were fairly well publicised in engineering journals of the day but no official picture is extant. I therefore asked my friend Col. Whitcombe to use these dimensions to draw a conjectural picture of her. We published it in the Journal of the Historical Model Railway Society and it appears facing page 102 with the Editor's permission.

Her boiler was pressed for the then very high figure of 100 lbs. per sq. inch. By 1852 her saddletank seems to have been giving trouble for Kirtley rebuilt her as a well-tank in January 1853. She was withdrawn from service in October 1861 and scrapped in July the following year, though there is a legend that her boiler only was scrapped and that her frames and motion had a prolonged existence in the No.221 well-tank which Kirtley built to replace her, and that 'Great Britain', thus rebuilt, soldiered up and down the Lickey till the turn of the century in company with her rebuilt stablemates 'Bristol' and 'Hercules'. 'Great Britain' was the first purpose built and successful Lickey banker and in her day created almost as great a sensation as 'Big Bertha' did in hers; for prominent engineers from all over the country came to watch her and to chat with her designer. Thereby hangs our final tale.

In 1844, for some reason which does not appear, McConnell was dissatisfied with his company house. Anyway in September 1844 he asked for, and obtained, permission to design and have built at the Company's expense, a house handier for the Works than the one he lived in with his sister. This house was built by James Bennett for £318 and in 1980 still stood, though dilapidated and vandalised. It was west of the track backing the abutments of the road overbridge at the station. It was finished in 1845 and McConnell had been in occupation about a year when the next event of interest happened.

A History of the Institute of Mechanical Engineers was written and published in 1947 by R. H. Parsons to celebrate their centenary. He relates therein how during the 1830/1840 period mechanical engineering had become a profession of considerable importance, and that one afternoon in the summer of 1846 a group of engineers were watching locomotive trials on the Lickey – or was it perhaps just the 'Great Britain'? – when a rain storm drove them to the shelter of a platelayers hut, when the discussion turned to the Institute of Civil Engineers; we can discount his story, borrowed from Smiles, of the Civil's treatment of George Stephenson because research has shown that it has no foundation in fact. The Institute of Civil Engineers was then the only society in the country which catered at all for engineers. Most of them belonged but it did not form a satisfactory forum for the discussion of their own peculiar problems. After the trials were over, those who could stay continued the conversation in McConnell's house at the foot of the incline. All agreed that the time had come for mechanical engineers to have an Institute of their own. McConnell offered his house as a venue for another meeting at

Captain Moorsom's white marker post at Lickey Summit.

When in 1841 McConnell got permission for his supplementary repair shed it was built as a lean-to against this wall and covered two tracks.

McConnell's house which he designed; built in 1844. The birthplace of the Institute of Mechanical Engineers.

Photographs by Rev. W. Awdry. The buildings were all due to be demolished in 1981.

which this should be the main item on the agenda. This was done and the Institute of Mechanical Engineers was born. The inaugural meeting was held in January 1847 in the Queens Hotel Birmingham, when George Stephenson was elected President and James Edward McConnell its first Chairman.

Earlier in that month McConnell had taken up his appointment at Wolverton. Kirtley absorbed the Birmingham and Bristol engines into Midland stock and closed Bromsgrove Works in favour of centralising all construction and repairs at Derby. In August of that year the Locomotive Works were let to Messrs Kinder and Johnson, coach builders of Worcester, for a rent of £316 a year which included McConnell's house. For some reason when the lease expired it was not renewed and Bromsgrove became one of the Midland Railway's most important Wagon Works.

The Locomotive Works had a short life of six years, but after an unpromising start they achieved two firsts in steam locomotive design: the first saddletank in March 1842 and, in June 1845 the first purpose built and successful Lickey Banker. A further claim to fame is that the world-wide Institute of Mechanical Engineers was conceived and born in McConnell's house at Bromsgrove Station. Three things of which Bromsgrove has every right to be proud.

Author's note. Thanks are due to Mr. E. H. Fowkes and his staff at the former B.T.H.R. Archives for help when collecting material used in this chapter (B.T.H.R. Archives are now at the Public Record Office, Kew).

W. Awdry

Chapter Nine

The Rise and Demise of Bromsgrove Guild

by Robert Pancheri

Photo by Roy Sayer with the co-operation of Buckingham Palace staff.
This ornament can seldom be seen on the gates as, except on special occasions, it is removed for safe keeping.

9

During the late 1890s, as part of a general plan to extend his curriculum beyond the strict confines of Greek and Latin, Herbert Millington, the Headmaster of Bromsgrove School, engaged the services of an art master. It was entirely against his better judgement, but he had yielded to the persuasion of one of his junior masters, R. G. Routh, who had joined the staff a year or two before and was intent on making the school prosperous and successful. The new art master already had some teaching posts – a day a week at the School of Art in Birmingham and three evening classes at the School of Science and Art in Bromsgrove, where he was head of the art department. His name was Walter Gilbert and he was second cousin to Sir Alfred Gilbert, notable at that time as the sculptor of the statue of Eros in Piccadilly Circus. But he was not Herbert Millington's sort of man – temperamental, vain, capricious, opinionated, argumentative and a dreadful dandy – and it was not long before he got the sack.

It was not the end of the world for Gilbert but it prompted him to look for another source of income. There was at this time a little furniture factory situated in an ancient brick building in Lamb's Lane, Charford, known as Moat Mill, run by two clever cabinet makers, Mr. Tapp and Mr. Armitage. They worked in the then fashionable style of the Arts and Crafts movement fostered by William Morris. Gilbert joined himself on to them to act as their agent and to promote their business, and he set up his first office there, in Moat Mill. It was a foundation he could build on. And build on it he did.

At the evening Art School in Bromsgrove he had two ladies on his staff who taught metalwork – the Miss Walfords. They too worked in the style of the Arts and Crafts Movement (Art Nouveau) in hand-beaten sheet metal copper, brass and silver with the pattern punched out from the back, 'repoussé', as it was called, with liberal insertion of semiprecious stones. A splendid and typical example of their work may be seen in the lectern at Tardebigge Church. The South African War Memorial in St. John's is also their work. These two Gilbert added to his agency and it was, incidentally, a piece of their work, a bronze reading lamp, which he showed in the British Pavilion in the Paris Exhibition in 1900 which was bought by the Austrian

Ambassador. Gilbert ensured for this news item the maximum possible publicity, and it was from then on that he began to call his little group the Bromsgrove Guild.

Meanwhile at the school in Birmingham there was a young Swiss jeweller, Louis Weingartner, who as part of his training had studied human anatomy and was a brilliant modeller. Gilbert used to give him little jobs from time to time, as occasion arose, models in clay or wax to be cast into bronze or lead, as well as carvings in ivory and small scale work, closer to a jeweller's profession. At this time both these men remained in their teaching posts.

Gilbert also got an agency for a Mr. Ludlow who had a fibrous plaster works at Puddle Wharf, and it is of interest that this establishment, which was operating before the Guild started, was still operating in the 1980s. At this stage there was no idea of bringing all these people under one roof or binding them together as a firm. The only link they had was through their sharing Gilbert's agency.

But in 1904 a curious chance was to change all that. Gilbert had in his class at Bromsgrove a daughter of the Earl of Plymouth, and at this time her father was having some alterations done to his house, Hewell Grange, by the fashionable architect Sir Aston Webb. Desiring perhaps to ingratiate herself with her teacher she invited Gilbert to come up to the Grange to meet Sir Aston when he was visiting there. It was at that meeting, in those favourable circumstances, that Gilbert was shown the plans for the forecourt of Buckingham Palace with the huge cast iron railings and gates with Coats of Arms and details in bronze. Gilbert did not let the chance slip. He got Weingartner at once to start a model for the great lock, with cherubs playing round it and one peering through the keyhole. These models, as displayed and explained to the architect by Mr. Gilbert, were sufficient to secure the order for Bromsgrove Guild.

Of course, at this time Gilbert had no factory and no money, but with this important commission on his books he soon found a backer. A Mr. McCandlish of Webheath agreed to put up the money and to form a limited company with himself and Gilbert as co-directors, registering themselves as 'Bromsgrove Guild Ltd.' As for a factory, the Bromsgrove Police had just built themselves a new Police Station in Ednall Lane and their old premises in Station Street were vacant and for sale. These the new company bought as they stood, on both sides of the street; and added to them those huge and horrible carapaces in corrugated iron so familiar to the locality during the twentieth century.

For labour they enlisted a Mr. Cowper from Coalbrookdale to set up a foundry and to bring in foundrymen from the Ironbridge district of Shropshire. Gilbert now began to bring his people into the new buildings, though he kept on, and expanded, his woodworking department at Moat Mill for many years after that. Weingartner gave up his teaching and moved to Bromsgrove. He was a very different character from Gilbert, being modest, shy, self-effacing and prodigiously industrious – the ideal mat for Gilbert to walk on. He meanwhile, always conceited, had now no hindrance to restrain his vanity. He moved from his house at the bottom end of Sidemoor to the old farm house at the bottom of Greenhill, Burcot, whence he would be driven to and from work in a black dogcart with yellow wheels, down Burcot Lane, along the Strand, down the High Street to Station Street, which was now beginning to be called Guild Hill. Everyone knew when the great Mr. Gilbert was coming to work and made way for him as if they recognised that the decisions he was pondering behind his gloomy brow affected all their lives.

Indeed there would have been at least some justification for such an attitude for Bromsgrove was at that time, as has been related earlier, a declining place with much unemployment; and that meant, more than it does in modern times, real poverty and starvation, and Gilbert had the ability to bring in work from all over England – and indeed from all over the world. In the brochure which he produced in 1907 he claimed to employ over one hundred people and he listed some of the work they had completed by that date. It is an impressive achievement for seven years' operations as may be seen from the extract from that brochure reproduced on page opposite.

Gilbert had other agents in the field to help bring in orders, notably one Cashmore in London; but Gilbert followed up all the leads himself and supervised all the work through its entire progress to completion, suggesting where necessary how it should be done and deciding who should do it. No small achievement that, to have built up such a firm from scratch in seven years!

The stained glass studio needs a special note because it never came under Gilbert's influence in quite the same way as the other departments did. Initially Gilbert persuaded Archibald John Davies, who was a tutor at the Bournville College of Art, and who concurrently had his own stained glass studio in Moseley, to become a member of the Guild. As principal, Davies then engaged among others Joseph Sanders, Albert Lemmon and Harry Rushbury. Rushbury was apprenticed to Davies but in the First

Extract from the 1907 brochure of the Bromsgrove Guild

Metalwork
Buckingham Palace Gates
Great Gates of Canada
Screens, lamps, gates and railings to Wellington Arch
Bronze lamps Buckingham Gate
Entrance Gates, Royal Infirmary, Newcastle-on-Tyne
Entrance Gates, Cartwright Memorial, Bradford
Bronze work to Royal Sussex Memorial
Lift enclosure and staircase of liner Lusitania
Bronze Catafalque, Sheffield Crematorium
Also electric fittings in:–
   Royal Naval College, Dartmouth
   The New War Office
   The New Admiralty
   The New Office of Public Works
   The Lusitania

Silver Trowels, Mallets, Keys etc. for:–
H.M. King Edward VII
The British Museum Extension
Royal Britannia Naval College
Royal College of Science
G.P.O. London
The War Office
Hearts of Oak Society

Medals etc. for:–
Auto Cycle Club of Britain
International Architectural Congress Badge 1906
Bromsgrove School Shooting Competition

Plasterwork
Cardiff Town Hall
Deptford Town Hall
Belfast City Hall
Woolwich Town Hall
London Sessions House
Birmingham University
Victoria and Albert Museum, South Kensington
Lancaster Town Hall
Royal Victoria Infirmary, Newcastle-on-Tyne
King Edward Sanatorium, Midhurst
The Lusitania

Leadwork
South Shields Town Hall
Northallerton County Buildings
North East Railway Buildings, York
Bristol Library
Eton College
Becketts Bank, York

Mosaic
Pediment in Hull School of Art

Stained Glass
Church of Messiah, Montreal

World War became a war artist. Later he was appointed Keeper of the Royal Academy Schools and received a knighthood.

Sanders left to take a commission in the Artist's Rifles and after the war set up his own studio in Lancaster. A good example of his work is the east window at Madresfield. Albert Lemmon left Davies' studio shortly after his war service and became Headmaster of Bromsgrove Art School. He also set up his own studio in the Strand. He has windows in most of the Bromsgrove churches and in very many churches around Birmingham. Being himself of High Church persuasion a great deal of his work is to be found in Anglo and Roman Catholic churches.

Though none of his work was for Bromsgrove churches, A. J. Davies produced stained glass windows for all over the world, including many churches and cathedrals in this country. His work in the Bromsgrove area can be seen at the Lickey and at Chaddesley Corbett. He had a distinctive style and his work can easily be recognised wherever it is found. His operations lay outside the ambit of Gilbert's activities so that his stained glass studio flourished for many years after Gilbert's time.

In the early days Gilbert drew most of his craftsmen – apart from the stained glass artists – from other European countries. It may be that the fact of employing Weingartner gave him the idea, or it may have been that he thought it would help to make his firm exclusive, or he may just have thought that foreigners were better. Certainly there was some wisdom in this because wage rates in England were at that time about double those on the Continent; tenpence (4p) an hour in London against half that sum in Paris and even less in other countries, so that he was easily able to choose the best and to persuade them to come here. In consequence besides Weingartner from Switzerland, Hubert and Pillon came from France, and Pancheri and Garscia from Italy. Garscia drowned himself in the Charford mill pond following an unhappy love affair. Pancheri and Pillon both married and settled for life in Bromsgrove. Added to these Sauer came from Hungary, Weisz from Germany, Voight from Austria, Bonnet from Spain and Meneggiu from Rumania. Polyglottal as they were their lingua franca was French and it is perhaps interesting to note that even Gilbert's wife was known as Madame Gilbert. Christian names were never used among them; indeed it was not the custom generally to do so in those days.

Madame Gilbert was a tall and beautiful woman, a brilliant hostess whose soirees were a feature of the local scene – a facility her husband was able to put to good use. One of the famous architects he used to visit in London was Sir Reginald Blomfield in whose offices he met a young architect, Arthur Bartlett, who was married, Gilbert discovered, to the sister of Mrs. Hendy, wife of the new headmaster of Bromsgrove School. Gilbert also knew that one of the curates of Bromsgrove Church, who was Priest-in-charge at Dodford, where the church was only a corrugated iron shack, had recently inherited a lot of money. His name was Whinfield and his father had left a fortune of ninety thousand pounds equally between himself and his two brothers. Shortly afterwards the youngest of the brothers died, unmarried and with no heirs, which would put, so Gilbert calculated, another fifteen thousand pounds in Mr. Whinfield's pocket; and this should be just enough to build a splendid little church for the parish. Precisely what wheels were set in motion we do not know, but it was not long before one of the famous soirees was graced by the presence of Mr. Whinfield and Mr. Bartlett, with the vicar of Bromsgrove and the Hendys and suitable elements of local society. Dodford Church was started the following year. Gilbert bought Bartlett a house, No. 1, Cedar Terrace, fixed him up with a fine drawing office, and tried to persuade him to stay. He stayed only to see his church completed, meanwhile building three houses in Bromsgrove, and then in 1912, went back to London.

Gilbert threw his tentacles far and wide. He had agencies in New Delhi, Cape Town, Valparaiso, New York and, most important of all, in Toronto. His agent there was a man called Wren, who had been an architect's assistant in the office of Tate & Herbert in Leicester. When an enquiry was received he would visit the site, meet the client, make a survey of the building and send the particulars back to Bromsgrove where Gilbert would assign somebody to prepare the designs and estimates which would be sent to the client. Gilbert's head designer at that time was a clever young Scot called Allen who had been an assistant to Sir Robert Lorrimer, and he had quite a team of designers and draughtsmen at his disposal. If the order was placed the job would be made in Bromsgrove, packed in crates, and shipped to Canada where Wren would engage local labour to fix it. This arrangement worked perfectly well with woodwork, or indeed metal or stained glass. But it could not be done with stone. It must have been that Gilbert had some important job in hand that decided him in 1912 to send his stonecarver, Weisz, to Canada. He sailed on the Titanic and was drowned. Weisz was one of the Guild's key men, and Gilbert was never able to replace him.

In 1914 the Great War put a stop to all the usual activities of the Guild, but Gilbert displayed a good deal of ingenuity, by taking on various kinds of war work and even produced some pressed copper plates for advertising.

When the war ended there was a tremendous demand for War Memorials with thousands upon thousands of letters to carve or to cast or to gild, and a huge boom in ecclesiastical work of all kinds; but, although nobody could see it at the time, the Guild's star was already beginning to set and in 1922 came Nemesis.

Some years before Gilbert had increased the size of his company by promoting three new members to the board; Allen, the chief designer, Cowper, the head of the foundry, and the Chief Secretary, Whewell. In those days Gilbert was travelling far and wide, away all week and only coming in at weekends to criticise the people who had been doing all the work. The firm was losing money and Gilbert's expenses were prodigious. He was incapable of economy, deaf to reason, and consumed with pride. It is not surprising that the other Directors took steps to protect their own interests – at least, one could see it like that. At all events, one weekend, when Gilbert returned, the Directors called a special meeting of the Board and accused Gilbert of obtaining work at their expense and farming it out secretly to other firms. It might have been true, unlikely though it seems, but it was a kangaroo court, Gilbert had no chance of defending himself, and he was voted off the Board.

People thought that the shock would kill him, that he should have been dismissed from his own company by men he had himself promoted to help him. For days he neither ate nor slept, but, at last, with his old friend Weingartner and a few others who had stayed loyal to him, he started up in business again in Birmingham. It was here, ironically enough, that he and Weingartner did the most important and spectacular job of their whole career together. This was the reredos in the Anglican Cathedral in Liverpool. Two details of the original plaster casts can be seen in the north-west corner of Hanbury Church.

The Guild meanwhile continued in Bromsgrove for many years; but Bromsgrove Guild without Gilbert was like Hamlet without the Prince of Denmark, and it declined progressively year by year until, by the end of the Second World War all that was left was one Director, one secretary, a telephone and a typewriter.

Looking back in hindsight over the story of the Guild one can see that the Brochure of 1907 really marked the apogee of its rocket-like ascent, and from then on we are watching a scintillating decline. As for the two principal actors some assessment has to be made. To assess Weingartner on his capacity as a sculptor would be both unkind and unwise, like assessing a circus horse on its capacity to run in the Derby. He was not that kind of animal. He was a gentle, kindly soul, who, in all his living took readily, as many people do not, to being told what to do; and this was Mr. Gilbert's special gift. The style of Art Nouveau moreover, which pervaded all the arts in Edwardian times, depended upon an integration of ornament with structure, or, as might be said, art with architecture. Gilbert's own, less happy, expression was 'art applied to architecture'. A profound understanding of the implications of such a style lay in Gilbert's very nature, and he was thus able to bring together an architect, for example, who wanted to say something, but did not know how to say it, with a modeller, who knew how to say almost anything, but did not know what to say. Gilbert understood absolutely what his client wanted, what his staff could do, and how to explain to them what needed to be done.

As for the famous gates they are still there. But the ornament around the great lock, which was their pièce de résistance was damaged when souvenir hunters stole some of the cherubs from it in about 1970. On royal instruction the whole ornament was then removed to save the risk of further loss. But before the Prince of Wales' wedding in 1981 moulds were made from those cherubs which were left and new ones cast in Delta Bronze so that the glory of the gates could be restored in time for the 'Wedding of the Century'. It is there upon those gates, on the ornament surrounding the lock, that the two names were inscribed together which briefly, and long ago, brought fame to Bromsgrove – Walter Gilbert and Louis Weingartner.

Chapter Ten

The Court Leet

by John Foster

The Court Leet and Court Baron

By Royal Charter Circa 1199

of the

Manor of Bromsgrove

10

King Alfred (871-899), he who reputedly burnt the cakes, may have been a poor cook but he was a clever administrator. He divided the country into shires, the shires into laths, and the laths into hundreds, the latter made up of ten tythings. The tything was a group of about ten families, each a pledge and a security for the others; they appointed from amongst their number a tythingman to answer for them all. To this day tythingmen are appointed to report to Bromsgrove's Court Leet at the 'View of frankpledge'.

The Court Leet is a survival from the manorial system introduced to this country by another well known King, William the Conqueror (1066). He commissioned the Domesday book which was completed in 1086 and in which the Manor of Bromsgrove is recorded. In broad outline the manorial system decreed that all land was owned by the king who granted the manors to his supporters or, perhaps, as in the case of Bromsgrove, a manor was retained for his own use. Thus the Manor of Bromsgrove was held in 'ancient desmesne'. Although in 1682 the Sovereign transferred it to Sir Thomas Windsor, (later Lord Plymouth) the privileges attached to this Royal manor could not be alienated and they continue to be enjoyed.

The courthouse was originally at the Lickey as the manor then extended from Grafton to Kings Norton. In 1564 a court was held at the Lickey, conducted by the Attorney General, for the express purpose of establishing separate manors for Bromsgrove and Kings Norton, though Queen Elizabeth was Lord of the Manor for both.

The government of the manor was in the hands of the Court Leet and one privilege of being 'Royal' was that the appointment of the Lord's steward – his chief agent – was subject to the approval of the court. The officers of the court were chosen by 'most voices' at a 'great court and view of frankpledge' held every autumn. This was a meeting of the freeholders in the manor at which the tythingmen reported on all the happenings within their 'yield' – so named because in addition to other duties they were also responsible for the collection of 'lewnes' or local taxes. The first election was that of bailiff, the chief officer of the court, followed by that of reeve. The reeve was originally responsible for the collection of the head rents for the Lord of the Manor. It was customary for the reeve to succeed to the office of bailiff. Other officers of the court were the 'affeerors', whose job it was to assess the proper amount of any fine which the court may have decided to impose. Other important officers were the equivalent of todays trading standards officers. In addition to aletasters there were breadweighers and searchers and sealers of leather. This last named appointment was necessary in Bromsgrove because Queen Elizabeth had licensed the town for the production of leather, a trade of importance to its prosperity. Many skinners, curriers, and tanners are recorded as having served the office of bailiff. A headborough and constables were appointed; and a bellman, who, besides acting as town crier, was required to clean the courtroom and the church steps and ring the market bell.

At the courts the steward, representing the Lord of the Manor, officially presides; but it is the bailiff who is responsible for summoning the court, executing its decisions and collecting all fines and other charges; the freeholders give judgement in all actions by 'most voices'. The customs of the manor which have subsisted, as the phrase goes, 'from the time when the memory of man runneth not to the contrary' are the basis of the law. The jurymen do not give the verdict, as juries do today, but act as wise men who give advice as to what those customs are. It will be from this body of men that the reeve, and the bailiff, will be chosen. After his year of office is over, the bailiff will become an ealdorman, and as such is relieved of other duties, though he should still support the bailiff when he 'walks the fair'

Those readers who seek more information about the working of the courts should refer to a publication of the Worcestershire Historical Society entitled 'The Court Rolls of the Manor of Bromsgrove and Kings Norton 1494 to 1504' and a lecture given in 1882 by W.A.Cotton to Members of the Bromsgrove Institute Debating and Mutual Improvement Society. This latter is reprinted in the Bromsgrove Messenger of 1910 and may be found in Notes and Queries available in Bromsgrove Public Library.

The bailiff had heavy responsibilities but he also had perks. The office was one of importance and during his year he was considered the first citizen of the town. He took commission from the sale of all wool which had to be weighed on scales he provided at the town hall; he also took the 'pitching penny' which shopkeepers were charged for putting out their stalls in front of their shops on fair day. Bromsgrove's fair is a charter fair granted by King John in 1199. But there is one traditional duty of the bailiff which, even today – perhaps especially today – he is not allowed to forget. He is

The picture opposite is from the collection of R. B. Brotherton; those on the following two pages from that of R. J. Richardson. They are early twentieth century and, thus, later than the period covered by most of this book; but they precede the motor age and consequently show Bromsgrove as it would have looked during much of the nineteenth century.

In the picture opposite taken in the Vicarage garden when Canon Noel Patterson was Bailiff in 1909 the members are as follows:
Back Row. G. H. Steele, R. Fowler, C. Wilden, F. Dutton, Jr., T. Jones, M. Spooner, Billy Albutt.
Standing. W. Woodward, J. B. Wilson, H. J. Phelps, E. Cotton, T. Fisher, W. Kimberley, Moses Nokes, E. Day, W. Weaver, J. Brown, J. Allcoat, G. Merriman.
Chairs. T. S. Ince, W. H. Wilson, W. Corbett, G. Brown, W. Hedges, Noel Patterson (Bailiff), Sam Saywell, Eustace Browning (Steward), Jos. Tilt, A. Roper.
Sitting on Ground. J. T. Taylor, A. B. Tilt, T. Roper, J. H. Beilby, A. H. Godsall, J. Clegg.

The Court Leet in 1909.

The two pages following show Bromsgrove on Fair Day 1902 and the procession at the Coronation celebrations for Edward VII. In the latter R. G. Routh, a master at Bromsgrove School since 1894, and Headmaster from 1913 to 1931, may be seen just to the left of the big drum. Both pictures were taken from the front of the Town Hall looking north.

required to entertain at his own expense the steward and officers of the court. In 1685 it is recorded that it cost Obadiah Alford £1;10. It costs more today! The following poem (origin unknown) suggests that the feasting was lavish, as indeed is confirmed by the menus of bailiff's dinners held in the early part of the twentieth century.

> Did he who of hard times complains,
> But once to Bromsgrove come,
> The generous plenty there that reigns,
> Would almost strike him dumb.
> The board is with the best supplied,
> Enough is to be done,
> And he who starts unsatisfied,
> The fault must be his own.
> At Whitsuntide, the happy time,
> Comes on, as people say,
> He's only guilty of a crime
> Who sober goes away.
> Then mark the jovial cause to prop,
> The bailiff's fix'd command,
> And may this custom never drop,
> As long as Bromsgrove stands.

Opposite is a copy of the menu of Bailiff Canon Paterson's dinner held in 1908 which further illustrates the point.

Canon Paterson had said when accepting the office "I shall go fearlessly for simplicity and it seems to me that we can have a good dinner without it being a luxurious one"!!

In opening the court the headborough proclaims " Oyez! Oyez! Oyez! all good people of Bromsgrove who have business to be heard before the Court Leet and Court Baron of Bromsgrove give your attention to the worthy steward or you will be amerced. God save the Queen !". To be amerced was to be fined or otherwise punished. The steward then swears in the jurors, their foreman first, saying: "You as foreman of this homage with the rest of your fellows shall enquire and true presentment make of all such things as shall be given to you in charge and all such matters as shall come to your knowledge presentable at this court. You shall present nothing out of hatred or malice nor conceal anything through fear favour or affection but in all things shall true and just presentment make according to the best of your understanding so help you God." The tythingmen report on all matters within their yield which might concern the court: complaints by one citizen against another; births, marriages and deaths; exchanges of land and so on.

"Then the goblets were crowned, and a health went round."--*lamb.*

Toasts.	Proposer.	Responder.
"His Most Gracious Majesty the King"	The Bailiff.	
"The Bishop and Clergy, & Ministers of all Denominations."	Dr. Underhill.	Rev. W. G. Whinfield.
Quartette -- "On the Banks of Allan Water" .. Parish Church Quartette.		
"The Naval and Military Forces of the Empire."	Alderman Day.	Dr. Beilby.
Song .. "Come into the Garden, Maud" ... Mr. T. Guest.		
"The Lord of the Manor."	Mr. Albert Eadie.	Mr. L. F. Lambert.
Quartette .. "Summer Eve."		
"The Bailiff."	Mr. Eugene H. Humphreys.	
Song ... "To Anthea." ... Mr. C. A. Hodson		
"The Town & Trade of Bromsgrove."	Mr. H. J. Phelps.	Mr. W. Corbett.
"The Reeve & Fore-man of the Jury."	Mr. T. Horton.	{ Mr. W. Hedges. Mr. S. Saywell.
Quartette .. { (a) "Evening Twilight" (b) "Absence."		
"The Visitors."	Mr. W. H. Wilson.	Mr. J. Campbell.

Menu.

Hors-d'œuvres.
Anchovies and Olives.

Soups.
Clear.   Tomato.

Fish.
Salmon & Cucumber.   Filleted Plaice & Tartare Sauce.

Entrées.
Fricassee of Pigeons.   Sweatbreads and Mushrooms.

Joints.
Sirloin of Beef.   Roast Lamb.

Poultry.
Ducklings and Peas.   Chickens and Asparagus.

Sweets.
Cherry Pudding.   Charlotte Russe.   Pastries.
Jellies and Creams.

Savouries.
Caviare Croustades.   Cheese Straws.

Cheese. ———— Salad.

Dessert. ————

Coffee.

WINES.
Sherry.   Still and Sparkling Hock.   Port.
Sparkling Moselle.

This was important as these events could all result in payments being due to the lord of the manor, such as a heriot payable on the death of a freeholder – usually the best beast. This form of death duty was first introduced by another famous King, Canute (995-1035).

The Court Leet was normally held four times a year, and the Court Baron which heard actions for recovery of debt, trespass and so on, was held every three weeks. Miscreants might be presented and amerced for a variety of offences including the throwing of slops into the street, parading a stallion between the hours of eleven o'clock and three, and singeing a pig in the street. If unable to pay a fine they might be put in the stocks which were often constructed so that they could also be used as a whipping post, another popular form of punishment. In 1681 twenty seven victuallers were presented to the court for breaking the assize of ale and eight bakers for breaking that of bread. As long ago as 1203 a law was passed for regulating the sale of bread and bakers who offended could be fined heavily and the bread given to the poor. Some examples from the court rolls may best illustrate the sort of cases which were heard.

A.D. 1489 Lykehay Great Court held there Monday next after Michaelmas, 5 Henry VII.

John Daffey complains that Elizabeth Berker on 20th June 1489 took and led away a horse of grey colour valued at ten shillings from his freehold within the jurisdiction of this court and imparked the same and detained it in the park until the Bailiff by virtue of a writ of replevin according to the custom of the manor delivered the said horse to the court at Lykehay whereby he (the plaintiff) is hurt and damaged to the extent of ten shillings.

A.D. 1490 Frank-Pledge, Thursday Pentecost 5 Henry VII

William Hawkes newly built a house upon the common at Moseley to the damage of the tenants without leave of the Lord.

A.D. 1502.

The tenant presented the death of William Barnsley whereby there falls to the Lady (the Queen) in the name of a heriot one feathered bed value three shillings and that Elizabeth Grace is his sister and next heir.

A.D. 1546 31st May. Lykehay Bromsgrove.

To this court came William Borworth who is an outlaw of the king and prayed that he may have liberty within his Lordship's land of Bromsgrove and Kings Norton to have and occupy all his goods and chattels according to the liberties of the same manor for this year and it is granted to him and he gives to the Queen as Lady of the Manor the fine of eightpence.

The powers of the court were eroded by Acts of Parliament passed between 1846 and 1925 which transferred the responsibilities of the manorial court to various other authorities. In 1977 the Administration of Justice Act abolished the right of Courts Leet to determine any legal matter, but in a rare recognition of the value of preserving tradition, refrained from abolishing the courts and allowed them to continue to transact such business as was traditional before the act became law. There is thus legal authority for Bromsgrove to continue the interesting customs, some of which have been observed for more than nine hundred years.

There is in existence a record of bailiffs of Bromsgrove going back as far as 1494, though it is only complete since 1733. The names of many old Bromsgrove families will be found amongst them. Many officers of the court gave lengthy service. Henry Albutt was Headborough and Town Crier from 1870 until 1918. W.H.Kimberley, who was Bailiff's Polebearer, submitted his resignation in 1934 at the age of 94 after fifty years service. Thomas Fisher, Searcher and Sealer of Leather and F. Alcock, a Tythingman, completed fifty years service in 1924 and 1928 respectively. More recently Cyril Nokes represented the court as Bailiff's Polebearer for twenty five consecutive years at the Henley in Arden Court Leet church service. The poles are an interesting part of the court's regalia, the first three of them being introduced in 1841. It is possible they were inspired by the pageantry of Queen Victoria's marriage to Albert the previous year. Two more were added later, one in the year of the Queen's diamond jubilee, 1897 and the other in 1902. They are carried in procession in front of the more important officers. When not in use they may be seen in a special showcase which is in the coffee bar at the Princess of Wales Hospital in Bromsgrove. They are inscribed with the date of origin and names of the bailiffs, reeves, and other officers before whom they have been carried.

As has been said Bromsgrove is a Royal manor, but for almost three hundred years the lordship was held by Lord Plymouth until his Worcestershire estate was sold in 1945. A substantial part of the estate was bought by Howard Bird who had been a tenant. He also acquired the lordship and he generously agreed to continue the ancient traditions of the court. On his death he bequeathed the lordship to his grandson, Christopher, who has since filled the role with great dignity.

Nowadays the court may best be observed when it carries out the assize of bread, leather and ale, and "walks" the fair. The proper date for this is midsummer day, but, in order to enable local people to enjoy the ceremony it is now held on the nearest Saturday. In 1983 a medieval street market was started on the same day when charity stalls are set up and entertainers roam the main street. The first royal charter for a fair was granted in 1199 by King John so that the people of Bromsgrove might "keep holiday and do honour to the patron saint of their parish of St. John the Baptist". So this has always been an opportunity for the townspeople to enjoy themselves and celebrate a bit of Bromsgrove's long history.

To some, though it is hoped not to those who have read thus far, it may seem that perpetuation of former ways of life has no meaning and no value; but let it not be forgotten that interesting picturesque customs reveal the spirit of the times which witnessed the laying of foundations on which we build. If the foundation is neglected the structure falls. On the foundation of Bygone Bromsgrove rests Bromsgrove Today and on which must be built Bromsgrove Tomorrow.

Bibliography and guide to further reading.

The Cotton Collection in Birmingham Public Library. This is the largest single source, collected by W. A. and John Cotton (over 100 vols.).

The Bromsgrove Messenger (1860 on). Available in Bromsgrove Public Library.

Notes and Queries 5 Vols. (1909, 1910, 1912, 1914 and 1927). These contain many of the *Bromsgrove Messenger's* historical articles.

History, Guide and Directory of Worcestershire by J. Bentley (1841).

Old Bromsgrove from 1642-1721, by E. A. Barnard (1926). A small booklet about Bromsgrove's Parish records.

Studies in Worcestershire History, ed. by E. A. Barnard (1938). This is a collection of articles by John Humphreys.

The Elizabethan Estate Book of Grafton Manor, by J. Humphreys ed. (1935). This dates from early in Elizabeth's reign giving a rare insight into life locally in Tudor times.

The Story of Bromsgrove, by W. G. Leadbetter (1946).

Bromsgrove and the Housmans, by J. Pugh (1974).

History of Worcestershire, by T. R. Nash (1781 - 1782).

Antiquities and Folklore, by J. Allies (1840).

The Old Straight Track, by A. Watkins (1925).

Worcestershire, by N. Pevsner (1968).

The Bromsgrove House, by F. W. B. Charles (Avoncroft 1967).

Worcestershire in English History, by A. MacDonald (1944).

Victoria County History, Worcestershire.

Bromsgrove – A Town Appraisal, Worcestershire County Council (1964).

Bromsgrove District Plan, Book 4. Conservation. Bromsgrove District Council (1976). Useful for dating High Street Buildings.

History of Bromsgrove Church, by W. A. Cotton (1881).

Rambles and Researches among Worcestershire Churches, by G. K. Stanton (1884).

St. Godwalds. A Parish and its People, by J. Grierson (1984).

The Bromsgrove Rovers' Centenary Book 1885-1985, by Bill Kings (1985).

Worcester Record Office for Manorial Rolls, enclosure and tithe award maps, wills and early photographs.

Other publications of The Bromsgrove Society are listed on the back cover.

1851 Census Records are on microfilm at the library of the North Worcestershire College, and the Worcester Record Office is a rich source of old maps, wills and photographs.

INDEX

Adams, J. 24
All Saints Church 40
Allen 123
Amiss, J. 53
Amphlett 44
Appleby................................18
Armitage 118
Avoncroft Museum 26
Bartlett, A.............................123
Bate, G.................................99
Battlefield Brook Ch.5, 25
Bennett, J. 113
Bird, H.................................137
Birmingham Canal Navigation..Ch. 7
Bischopp, G. D. 109
Blew, Misses 51
Blomfield, Sir R. 74,122
Boulders 20
Brewster, J. & E. 78
Bridgman, J. 80
Bromsgrove Devil 29
Bromsgrove Fair..............22, 23
Bromsgrove Flood 16
Bromsgrove Guild ....Ch. 9
Bromsgrove House...............26
Bromsgrove Messenger 40
Bromsgrove School......25, 47, 57, 72
Brooke, F. 81
Broom House 54
Brown J. 55
Buckingham Palace Gates 119
Bury, E 107
Cade, Jack 64
Charles I 28
Charles II 25,28
Cholera 50
Church, Dr 102
Clapton, J 80
Clegg's Entry.........................16

Clowes, J. 95
Coaches................................16, 51
Collett, J 85
Collis, Dr. 53, 57
Congregational Chapel...........32, 46
Cook, Mrs. and Jane 51
Cookes, Sir Thomas 25, 29, 72
Cooper, Dr. T. 95
Corbett, W. 82
Cordell 48
Cottage Hospital 29
Cotton, W. A. 31, 40
Cotton, John 40
Cotton Mill 23, 50, 78
Court Leet ....Ch. 10
Cowper, G. E. 120
Crane, J. 17, 23, 42
Creuze 109
Crossley, W. 96
Crown Close 14
Cutler 44
Davenal House 39
Davies, A.J. 120
Day, T. 40
Dell 47
Dipple, G. 45
Dixon, T. & M. 97
Dodd, M. 53
Domesday Book 14, 82
Donahue, J. 106
Dufill 53
Edwards, T 61
Ethelflaeda 12
Fawke, Sgt. 59
Field....................................51
Finney 77
Fisher, T...............................46
Fletcher, Dr. G. 43, 58
Fletcher, Dr. T. S..............46, 49, 57

Fletcher (Toyshop).......................48
Francis 44
Frayne, Mrs. 48
Freemasons 46
Garscia 122
Gas Light Co. 45
Gilbert, R. 53
Gilbert, W. ....Ch. 9
Gillespy 48
Goddard 102
Godfrey. I. 78
Godsall, J. W. 82
Goodwin, W. H. 111
Grafton Manor ....Ch. 3
Green, W. 39
Green, Mrs.................................51
Greening, J. & W. 47
Griffin....................................44
Gunpowder Plot 66, 71
Gwynn, W. 105
Habington..................................66
Haines, Dr. 46
Haines, (Apothecary)......................48
Haines. (Miller) 77
Harrison, T. 77
Hartle, W. 53
Harvington Hall 67
Hedges, W. 81
Hewell Grange 119
Hill, W. 51
Hinksman, A. 70
Holyoake 18, 29
Horton, Dr. 46, 51, 53
Housman, A. E 24, 57
Housman, L. 24
Housman, Rev. T. 47
Humphreys, J. 57
Huxley, A. 45
Ince, H....................................39

Inns and Taverns
  Lower Dolphin
  White Swan   }..................48
  Bell
  Black Cross 25
  Britannia 26
  Cattle Market Tavern
  Old Sow and Pigs   }....31, 51
  Dunklin's Mug House
  Coach and Horses 51
  Crabmill.........................40, 80
  Crown Inn 43
  Dog and Pheasant 26
  Dragoon 54
  George Inn 22
  Golden Cross 27, 46
  Golden Lion 27
  Green Dragon 48
  Halfway House........................99
  Hop Pole Inn 28, 43
  Hundred House 43
  Leg of Mutton 24
  Mitre 35
  Navigation 98
  Queens Head
  Blacksmiths Arms }...............99
  Queens Head..........................35
  Red Lion 53
  Roebuck 51
  Sampson 26
  Shoulder of Mutton 24
  Star and Garter 46
  Turk's Head..........................26
  Unicorn..............................31
  Upper Dolphin 53
  Vigo................................109
  Wheatsheaf 26
Inshaw, J. 102
Jakeman, J. 53

Jefferies 44
Jenner, Rev, C. H. 58
Jessop, W.......................................96
Jones, T...80
Keep, K. 51
Kings, Mrs. 51
Kings, J. 61
Knight, Miss 48
Knight, J.......................................79
Lacey, J...49
Lambe, C. H. 82
Lammas 78
Leadbetter, J.................................60
Lemmon, A. 120
Lickey Incline ....Ch. 8
Llewellyn, W. 45, 80
Lloyds Bank 31
Ludlow 119
Lyttleton 14, 29, 66
Manorial Court House 129, 136
Manningly, T..................................39
Marcus 56
Market 18
Martin, W. 81
Matthews, W.................................80
Maund, B. 16, 44, 47
McCandlish................................119
McConnell, J. E...................107, 109
Merrel, Steerer............................99
Methodists 40
Mills ....Ch. 5
Millington, H. 118
Milton, J......................................81
Morris, J. & J. 48
Munslow 48
Nailers and nailing ....Ch. 6
National School 14, 56
Naylor...70
Nokes, Moses 49

Norris Engines ....Ch. 8
O'Connor, Feargus 27
Oddfellows 61
Oldcorne, Father 67
Overton, W. H...............................78
Pagett 74
Pancheri, C.................................122
Parkes 49
Parry, J..80
Pearsall, W. 78
Perkins, E. 46
Perkins, Martha 53
Perry Hall 24
Pillon...122
Plymouth ....See Windsor
Price, Miss Mary 59
Prosser 51
Rainscourt's 31, 49
Rectory Manor House 35
Rennie, Sir J. 96
Richardson, T. H...........................80
Richmond 53
Roberts, F.....................................81
Robeson...................................46, 49
Rogers...45
Roman Road 20
Rose, John 59
Rose, Joseph 58, 85
Rose, W. 48, 59
Rotton, J.......................................78
Routh, R. G................................118
Rushberry, H 120
Rutherford, J 102
Russon 54
Salt Track 20
Sanders, B. H. 48
Sanders, Benjamin 79, 85
Sanders, James.............................79
Sanders, Joseph 120

Sanders, Miss Mary 51
Sanders, R. 35
Saywell, L. T. 57
Scaife, T. 102
Scott, Sir G. 70
Scroxton, J. H. 47
Sherrat, T. 95
Simmons, H. E. S. 82
Simms 47
Smith, C. 45
Smith, J. 80
Snape, J. 95
Spadesbourne Brook ....Ch. 5
St. John's Church ....Ch. 4
St. John's Sunday School 56
St. Peter's Church 67
Stafford, Sir H 12, 64
Stafford, Lady Alianora 14
Steedman 44
Stephenson, G. 113
Talbot, Sir G. 28, 64
Talbot, Elizabeth 65
Talbot, J 65
Tandy's Tannery 37
Tapp 118
Taylor, W 82
Thomas, T. D. 45
Thompson, T 99
Tinsley, Eliza 39
Tithe Barn 31
Toll Houses 43
Town Hall 20
Town Mill 32, 53, 81
Troth, C 85
Tudor 48

Van Beurle, H 110
Veal, J 80
Vicarage 14
Wagstaff, S 59
Walford, Misses 118
Wall, Father 67
Walworth 109
Ward 44
Warwick Hall 54
Watt Close 23
Watton, W. 49
Weaver, J. 80
Weaver, W 46
Webb, Sir Aston 119
Webley 49
Weighing Machine 37
Weingartner, L 119
Weisz 122
Wesley, J 40
Wetherall 112
Whewell 124
Whinfield, Rev 123
White, T 58
Wildsmith 48
Wilson, J. B 53
Wilson, H 80
Windsor, Earl Plymouth ..66, 119, 129
Woodcock 48
Woodhouse, J 95
Workhouse, (old) 37, 61
Workhouse, (Union) 39
Worsey, J 78
Wright, Sgt. ....Ch. 1, Title Page
Wyntour 66
York, I. 106